Ready, Set, Retire!

How Much Money You Need
&
The TAX-SMART Way To Get It & Keep It

J. William Brimacombe

Financial Freedom Press
P. O. Box 6285
Bend, Oregon 97708-6285
(800) 382-6936

Jacket Design by Design of the Times
Printed in the United States of America

Brimacombe, J. William.
Ready, Set, Retire!: How Much Money You Need & The TAX-SMART Way To Get It & Keep It / by J. William Brimacombe.
Includes glossary. Includes index.
1. Finance, personal. 2. Retirement income — planning.

ISBN 0-9641532-3-8
332.024'01—dc20   Library of Congress Number 94-66841

For information on ordering,
see the form in the back of this book.

Financial Freedom Press books are available for educational, business and sales promotional use and may be purchased in bulk at special discounts. For information, contact the Special Markets Department at the address below.

Financial Freedom Press
P. O. Box 6285
Bend, Oregon 97708-6285
(800) 382-6936

To the 90+% of Americans who
will fail to achieve financial independence
before they retire
if they don't take action NOW!

Contents

Revenue Bonds • Defaults • Impact On Social Security
Income To Be Taxed • Versus Taxable Investments •
After-Tax Yield To Maturity • Yield Formulas

About the Author

J. William Brimacombe is the president of Financial Security Corporation, a consulting firm that specializes in teaching tax-smart investment strategies through educational seminars. Bill brings to the task both the educational background of advanced degrees in accounting and finance and the experience of over thirty years as an investor, accountant, investment consultant and manager. With both uncommon sense and a well-developed sense of humor, Bill shows the seemingly elusive goal of success in investments can be surprisingly easy. He's a frequent guest on financial shows, and a much in-demand speaker.

Bill escaped from the Congressional Revenue Hunters in his hometown, Washington, D.C., and now pursues assorted family adventures that include swimming, hiking, skiing, canoeing and white-water rafting along with his wife, Cathy, and children, Christie and Scott.

*"We should all be concerned about the future
because we will have to spend
the rest of our lives there. "*
— *Charles Kettering*

Preface

Countless people have asked me for help in achieving their financial goals. Usually, they come to me with a mixture of confusion and apprehension.

Confusion is normal. There are hundreds of periodicals, books, videos, infomercials — you name it — promising to show you the way to financial success. Some even promise to reveal the "secrets" to financial freedom. To make matters worse, much of this information — reliable and otherwise — is presented in a way that can best be described as difficult, dry and dull. Is it for enlightenment or sedation? You be the judge!

Then there's the problem of apprehension. And why shouldn't people be hesitant about investing, after all? We're served a daily media diet of financial scandals and scams, unscrupulous "financial advisors," deals gone sour, and people left destitute. Combine that with no educational background or personal experience in investments and you have the perfect recipe for fear and worry.

Too often, unfortunately, this confusion and apprehension causes people to do the one thing they can't afford to do with their money — nothing! Instead of investing for their long-term goals, most people merely "park" their money in low-yielding, ultra-conservative, insured accounts. Indeed, these accounts are guaranteed to return dollars. But those *future* dollars will have less purchasing power, after taxes and inflation are considered, than the dollars that are "parked" today. If people do this long enough, they'll probably never achieve financial independence. Worse, they'll run out of money long before they die.

I hope this book will clear up some of the confusion you may have about investments. I hope that as you understand investments better, you will be less apprehensive about pulling out of your financial "parking place" and truly investing to achieve your important long-term financial goals.

Bill Brimacombe

1
The Buck Stops With You!

The Great Retirement Funding Responsibility Shifts

Parts I and II

Did you ever wonder why all of those 19th century mid-west farmhouses were so big? Or how about those late 19th century Victorian beauties that still grace the avenues of most small towns in America? Are Americans shrinking? If not, then why do houses today seem so much smaller?

I may not be able to prove it, but I'll bet the answers to these questions lie in the changing *nature* of American families and not their *stature*. In the 19th century, families included kids, parents, grandparents even aunts, uncles, great-grandparents, great-aunts and great-uncles. It was common for them all to live under the same, large roof. As children grew up and their parents grew old, everyone stayed together. All family members helped with chores. And all pitched in what resources they had to support the entire, extended family.

Retirement in those earlier days didn't happen at a specific point in time. It was a gradual change, from a more active to a less active contribution to the family's financial well-being. Aging parents weren't expected to have salted away enough money to provide for independent living arrangements. They were expected to continue to live in the same house as the rest of the family.

Part I - From *Family* To *Government* & *Industry*

The Great Depression of the 1930s changed all that. Large numbers of people were out of work in every city and hamlet throughout the land. There were massive migrations of impoverished people leaving farms that had been in families for generations. Nuclear families of parents and children couldn't provide for themselves. How could they be expected to provide for aging grandparents and other older relatives?

The idea of "Old Age and Survivors Insurance" was born. The government developed the vast Social

Security system to fill the void. Thus began the *First Great Retirement Funding Responsibility Shift*. Families who were no longer able to provide for their aged relatives in retirement could now shift that responsibility to Social Security.

As time passes, government programs grow (some would say bloat!). Social Security was conceived as a government program to provide for the indigent elderly. Now it has grown to include virtually every retired person in America, regardless of their need for income assistance.

This shifting of responsibility for retirement funding from the family to governmental institutions was accompanied by the emergence of Employer-Funded Retirement Plans. Pension benefits became a principal issue of collective bargaining between unions and management. In the white collar ranks and executive suites, pension benefits became major "perks" that were used both to attract new talent and to retain the valued employees already on board.

Pension plans usually took the form of defined benefit plans. Through these plans, companies promised to pay a specified (i.e. defined) amount of money (i.e. benefit) to an employee during each of his or her retirement years.

This completed the First Great Retirement Funding Responsibility Shift — the shift from the family to institutions, both governmental and corporate.

Part II - From *Government & Industry* To *YOU!*

Now, in the last quarter of the 20th century, we see the Second Great Retirement Funding Responsibility Shift occurring. Due to what I would politely describe as a lack of political will in the face of economic reality, the Social Security system has been expanded so far that it has essentially run out of money. Social Security benefits for current retirees don't come from the earnings they set aside in earlier years. In fact, they never have! Instead, benefits for current retirees come from the Social Security taxes paid by those still working. What is so alarming is that as the American population ages, the ratio of people still working to those drawing retirement benefits is shrinking. So the shortfall in the Social Security system is likely to get worse, not better.

What's more, current benefits only cover about one-third of a retiree's income requirements. The balance must come from employer-provided retirement benefits and personal retirement savings.

But watch out! Employers don't have the money to fund retirement plans, either. The competitive pressures of the world economy have rippled through companies in America both large and small. Corporate "perks" have given way to downsizing and restructuring. The "fat and happy" have become "lean and mean" or extinct. Defined *benefit* plans — funded by the company, even if the company is losing money — have faded. Meanwhile, defined *contribution* plans have grown. These plans are funded by the company only if the company is making money. If the company isn't making money, there's no money put into the pension plan. What's worse, many companies have gotten out of the business of funding retirement plans almost entirely. Instead, they only offer employees the opportunity to contribute, out of their paychecks, to 401(k) plans.

These newer retirement plans also take the responsibility for managing the retirement funds out of the hands of the company. Now, employees at every level are being told to make their own investment decisions — and to enjoy or suffer the consequences.

This Second Great Retirement Funding Responsibility Shift is clear. No longer will governmental and corporate institutions take responsibility for funding an individual's retirement. This responsibility has now shifted directly to the individual. *The Buck Stops With You!*

This dramatic Second Shift is coming at a particularly terrible time. Families that have scattered to the far corners of the country will find it extremely difficult to provide for aging relatives. My family is probably typical in that we have relatives scattered from Oregon and California in the west, to Minnesota, Michigan and Iowa in the mid-west, and to Maryland, Virginia and Washington, D.C. in the east. Putting us back together under the same roof to provide for retirement needs would be impossible — not to mention *extremely* crowded!

At the same time, working family members are laboring under the most expensive Social Security tax bite ever. Gone are the days when even minimum wage workers could look forward to paychecks early in the year that didn't have Social Security taxes (FICA) taken out. Now, FICA taxes come out of incomes as high as $60,000+ (and that dollar amount will increase each year as wages increase with inflation). What's more, Medicare taxes can't be escaped at all, since there's no limit on the earnings subject to the tax.

The burden on young people today is enormous. Many of them have large outstanding student loans due to soaring college tuition costs. Inflation in housing costs has also hit the young particularly hard. Now, while working under sharply higher taxes, that dream of home ownership has faded for many. Given all of this, can the young be expected to provide for their elderly relatives' retirement needs? I, for one, don't think so.

If young, working people can't be expected to help provide for their elderly relatives' retirement needs, and the government and employers don't have the money, then it is up to the elderly themselves.

Senior citizens are also changing. For one thing, people are living a lot longer than in earlier times. A person born in 1930 had a life expectancy of 59.7 years. By 1970, that figure had leaped to 70.8 years. Now, life expectancy is 75.4 years.

As a result, the percentage of the population that is age 65 or older is growing rapidly. In 1930, the 65 and over group represented only 5.4% of the population. By 1970, the percentage had grown to 9.9%. Now, 12.6% of the population is 65 or older. By 2010, U.S. Census projections show that 14% of the population will be 65 or older. By that time, Willard Scott will need his own half hour show each day just to read the names of everyone celebrating 100th birthdays!

Retirees, both current and future, are now facing a major challenge. They must stretch shrinking retirement funds over a lengthening life expectancy. To meet this challenge, people need investment strategies that will minimize the effects of inflation and taxes. For most people, simply putting their retirement nest egg in federally insured 3-month certificates of deposit at the bank won't work. If taxes don't eat up the interest, inflation surely will.

The retirement nest egg will simply run out! What may have lasted for the 1930 life expectancy of 59.7 years clearly won't last for the 75.4 year life expectancy of the 1990's.

In later chapters, I'll discuss the challenge of providing for your own retirement with very little help from your government, employer or family. And I'll show you ways the challenge can be met.

Before that, however, we need to develop a better understanding of the term "risk." The next chapter should help.

*"Life is risky.
No one gets out alive!"*
— *Anon.*

2
Understanding Risk

" ☼ ⅔#&*!! Hey, idiot! Get outta my way!"
"Bang! Crunch! ⋓#@$%! You jerk!"

We're all familiar with the risk of getting hurt. Whether dodging nasty comments or reckless drivers, we've all grown up aware of emotional and physical threats.

Over the years, we develop strategies for dealing with these threats. We learn to drive defensively, for example. We wear protective helmets when playing contact sports. We develop thicker skins. We even learn to avoid what we've learned to identify as "dangerous" activities.

But what about investment risk? The financial world can't even agree on a definition. There are some people who might say that an investment is risky if it isn't insured. These are comfort-seeking souls whose idea of a big risk might be switching to gel toothpaste! They smile like Cheshire cats and nod like wisemen when someone suggests they don't really need to have all their money insured. "You must be crazy," they'll say, as if putting money somewhere other than a federally insured vault, with three-foot thick walls, is the equivalent of bungee-jumping! These folks have a mental library of stories about friends and relatives who've "lost everything!" in some investment scheme. They'll gleefully trot out the story about Uncle Harvey, who put his money into a mining stock in the Yukon and ended up papering his den with the stock certificates. They'll tell you how their parents (their grandparents, or they themselves) "got clobbered" in 1990 or 1987, or 1973-74, or whenever it was that they, their friends or relatives panicked and sold out at the bottom of a market swing.

With these fearful folks, there is no middle ground. An investment is either insured or very risky; and only fools would put their money in something that's risky, right?

Their definition of risk goes *beyond* logic. They define risk in terms of emotional blacks and whites. Insured investments aren't risky. Everything else is. "'Nuff said! No more discussion needed!" they'll say.

Let's face it. That's just some people's nature. On the other hand, *most* people try to apply logic to their definition of risk. Most people simply want some assurance they'll get their dollars back when they invest. Along the way, they hope they'll earn some income from the investment and/or they hope that it will grow at a reasonable rate during the time it is invested. For example, when they invest $10,000 for

5 years, they expect they'll earn some income for those 5 years. They also hope they'll get their $10,000 back at the end of those 5 years. And these are perfectly understandable, reasonable goals!

But here's the rub. For these people, risk is often measured in terms of how likely it is that they'll get their $10,000 back. Using this definition, if the return of their $10,000 is insured, there's virtually no risk. If similar, uninsured investments have a long history of being able to return the full $10,000, then there may be some risk, but very little. If there's a significant chance that the investment may return either more than or less than $10,000, then there's more risk.

This definition of risk has the advantage of being easy to understand. At the same time, it has the disadvantage of being very misleading.

Let me explain with an example. If you put $10,000 into a federally-insured bank account that earns 3% interest, you'll earn $300 in interest next year. At the end of that time, the bank will give you back your $10,000. Simple, right?! Right!

Low risk, right? Wrong!!!

First, you'll have to pay income tax on the $300 in interest that the bank pays you each year. So your $300 is really only $216 ($300 minus $84 in federal income taxes for a taxpayer in the 28% federal income tax bracket). I've ignored the effect of state and local income taxes that could whack away another $30 or so off the money you actually get to keep!

Second, we have to calculate the effect of inflation. Remember that when you deposited the $10,000 in the bank, you gave up the purchasing power of $10,000. What did the bank give you back at the end of the year? The bank gave you 10,000 *dollars*, NOT the same *purchasing power* as the $10,000 you started with. At just 4.5% inflation (that's what inflation has averaged over the last 35-40 years), the $10,000 you deposited would need to grow to $10,450 just to give you the same purchasing power that you started with one year earlier. So what did the bank give you? And what did you need to get back just to stay even with inflation, after taxes?

Required to Stay Even With Inflation $10,450

Less: Rec'd From Bank:	Principal	$10,000	
	Interest	300	
Less: Income Taxes		(84)	10,216

Loss from the Bank: $ 234

As the illustration shows, you needed $10,450 *just to stay even with inflation*, after taxes! But the bank gave you only $10,216, after taxes. That's a loss in purchasing power of $234!

So now we need to develop a *Purchasing Power* definition of risk that deals with these economic realities, including taxes and inflation. Here it is:

Risk is the possibility that an investment will give us less future purchasing power than we started with, after deducting taxes and the effects of inflation.

Using this definition, we should be interested only in investments that will give us future purchasing power, after taxes and inflation, that is greater than the purchasing power that we're investing today. Any investment that fails to give us an increase in future purchasing power should be viewed as risky.

Now let's apply this *Purchasing Power* definition of risk. As we can see below, investments that are traditionally viewed as low risk, are really rather risky:

Risk Level	Traditional View of Risk	*Purchasing Power* View of Risk
Lowest	Bank Savings Accounts	Foreign Common Stocks
	Certificates of Deposit	Small Company Common Stks
	U.S. Treasury Bills	Blue Chip Common Stocks
	U.S. Treasury Notes	Investment Real Estate
	U.S. Treasury Bonds	Low Grade Corp Bonds
	Insured Muni. Bonds	Med. Grade Corp Bonds
	Uninsured Muni. Bonds	High Grade Corp Bonds
	High Grade Corp Bonds	Uninsured Muni. Bonds
	Med. Grade Corp Bds	Insured Muni. Bonds
	Low Grade Corp Bonds	U.S. Treasury Bonds
	Investment Real Estate	U.S. Treasury Notes
	Blue Chip Stocks	U.S. Treasury Bills
	Small Company Stocks	Certificates of Deposit
Highest	Foreign Common Stocks	Bank Savings Accounts

Most investments traditionally thought of as "safe," like bank savings accounts, certificates of deposit, U.S. Treasury securities, and insured municipal bonds, really aren't safe using our *Purchasing Power* definition of risk. These investments have usually failed to produce an increase in purchasing power, after deducting taxes and inflation.

To illustrate this, look at the chart on the next page that compares the growth of a $100 investment in various securities with the change in the cost of living.

Growth of a $100 Investment
After Taxes For 28% Tax Bracket
January 1, 1969 - December 31, 1993

Common Stocks ++++++++++++++++++++++++++ $ 875
Treasury Bills ++++++++++++ $ 417
Cost of Living ++++++++++++ $ 411

So what should an investor do? I think you must always ask how much income and capital appreciation an investment is likely to provide, after deducting taxes and inflation. The goal should be to invest as little as possible in things that don't provide for an increase in purchasing power at the end of the investment period.

Of course, emergency funds for things like medical emergencies, the deductible amount on an auto insurance policy, etc., should be kept in places where instant access to dollars is assured. Bank savings accounts and money market funds are appropriate for such emergency funds.

It makes little sense, however, to invest long-term funds in such places. Why lose purchasing power on your long-term funds? Retirement funds are clearly long-term. Even a 70 year old retiree should view a retirement nest egg as long term, since the average 70 year old has a 10-25 year life expectancy. That's long term!

But what about the disturbing price fluctuations of

some types of assets? For example, bonds go up in price when interest rates drop. When interest rates go up, however, the price of existing bonds goes down. Sure, if you hold a bond to maturity, the price will be the same as the face amount you originally bought. In the meantime, from the time you buy it until the time it matures, a bond's price will bounce like a yo-yo.

Stocks bounce around, too. Just listen to the nightly news on TV and you'll hear about the stock market "plunging" and "soaring." For the life of me, I can't see why a rise of 1% in the stock market is "soaring," yet that's what newspeople call a 40 point increase in the Dow Jones Industrial Average (DJI). It's even worse when the stock market drops. "Heard-on-the-street" interviews appear when the stock market "plunges" just 2.5% (100 points on the DJI). "How will you survive the wipe-out?" a breathless reporter asks. Talking-head expert commentators are summoned to "explain the disaster."

Let's face it, investment securities and properties change in price every day. In the case of investment properties, it's difficult to see these daily changes. There's no centralized price quotation facility available to the general public. Even real estate agents have to wait several weeks between a sale and a settlement before they know actual prices.

Stock market price quotations, on the other hand,

are readily available almost anywhere in the world. In fact, it's hard to escape them. Virtually every daily newspaper reports stock prices. Stock market reports fill the radio airwaves several times a day on many stations. You can call a local telephone number for price quotes through the facilities of newspapers across the country. Every city, town and village also has its share of brokerage firms who'll gladly give you price quotations.

Many will agree with me that the availability of information about stock price fluctuations can give people a false impression. The mere fact that they're readily available and widely published may give them more importance than they deserve. "If the newspaper prints stock prices every day, somebody must think they're important. The newspaper wouldn't publish them, otherwise." So goes the reasoning.

It's too bad that the daily fluctuations of stock prices obscure the overall, long-term upward trend of stock prices. *That upward trend has averaged over 10% per year for the past 25 years*, but few people are probably aware of it. What people are aware of is that stock prices "plunge" and "soar."

So how should you deal with the discomfort most people feel from the "plunging" and "soaring?" For years, I've advised people to follow five simple steps in their investments. If followed, you should be able to sleep quite comfortably through periods of all but the most extreme fluctuations in stock prices.

Five Steps For Comfortable Investing

1. **Diversify your investments**. "Don't put all your eggs in one basket," your mother told you. And you know, Mom was right. Spread your risks. It's obvious that owning only one stock won't give you adequate diversification. I don't think a stock or bond portfolio should have more than 5% in any single security, for example.

    Investing your money in only one mutual fund isn't sufficient, either. Sure, the fund may own dozens of different stocks. But those stocks may be from only a handful of different industries. If those few industries do well, so does your investment portfolio. If not, you sink, too. To protect yourself, I think you need to own at least five different mutual funds:

i.   Large company stock fund for growth
ii.   Small company stock fund for growth
iii.   International stock fund
iv.   Combination growth and income fund
v.   Bond fund (corporate, U.S. Government or municipal, depending on a person's individual circumstances)

2.   **Stretch your investment time frame.** Even a diversified portfolio of securities will fluctuate widely if you look at only one-year time frames. But as I show below, the differences in the range of performance from one *five-year* period to another have been less than half the differences of *one-year* periods. Stretch that to a *twenty-year* time frame, and there's been an even smaller amount of volatility. Since your financial goals are long-term in nature, try to focus on the long-term performance of your portfolio, not the day-to-day fluctuations.

The chart below shows the results of investing in the stock market (represented by the Standard & Poor's 500 Index) for various time periods from 1928 through 1993. During that time, there were 65 1-year periods, 61 5-year periods, 56 10-year periods, and 46 20-year periods.

If you had only invested for one year at a time, for example, you could have had a gain as great as +54% or a loss as great as -43%. That's a wide range of possibilities. If you had invested for at least 5 years each time, your worst loss would have been -12%

Range of Gain/Loss for S&P 500 — 1928-1993
 1 Year   -43% ★★★★★★★★★★★★★★★┼★★★★★★★★★★★★★★★★★★ +54%
 5 Years   -12% ★★★★┼★★★★★★★★ +24%
 10 Years   - 1% ┝★★★★★★ +20%
 20 Years   - 3% ┿★★★★★★ +17%

3.   **Use professional management**. Everyone will agree, probably, that emotions will hurt a person's investment performance. The depression you feel from a recent death in your family should not cause you to be panicked about your investments. Likewise, personal success on the golf course shouldn't be translated into a burst of speculative fervor in your portfolio.

Hire a professional money manager for your money. A professional can be objective even when you're not. A mutual fund, for example, can provide this professional money management for a very reasonable cost. And invest-ment minimums are low enough for many funds to allow investments of only $250.

4. **Just say "No to News."** Tune out news of short-term market fluctuations. When a TV commentator starts reporting the "plunging" and "soaring" of the stock market, tune it out. Stop listening to such short-term reports.

    Remember, you're a long-term investor. You're diversified. You use professional mon-ey management. These short-term reports simply don't apply to you. "What do these reports have to do with making money, any-way?" some might ask. The wise investor's answer is "Nothing!"

5. **Don't follow the day-to-day performance of your investments.** "A watched pot never boils," the old cliché says. And it certainly applies to investments. Review your portfolio every 6 months or once a year. That's all you really need to do.

    Your review isn't so much to determine winners and losers in your portfolio. The real purpose of your review is to see if your portfolio is allocated in a way that fits your goals.

Toward this end, I've listed below some asset allocations you might want to consider:

Conservative Investor

Age	Cash	Bonds	Stocks	Real Estate
20s	80%	20%	0%	0%
30s	10%	35%	45%	10%
40s	5%	35%	50%	10%
50s	5%	40%	50%	5%
60s	10%	60%	30%	0%
70+s	10%	60%	30%	0%

Moderate Investor

Age	Cash	Bonds	Stocks	Real Estate
20s	80%	15%	5%	0%
30s	10%	30%	50%	10%
40s	5%	30%	50%	15%
50s	5%	35%	50%	10%
60s	5%	55%	35%	5%
70+s	10%	55%	35%	0%

Aggressive Investor

Age	Cash	Bonds	Stocks	Real Estate
20s	80%	10%	10%	0%
30s	10%	25%	55%	10%
40s	5%	25%	55%	15%
50s	5%	30%	50%	15%
60s	5%	45%	45%	5%
70+s	5%	55%	40%	0%

Ask a financial professional for help in designing an appropriate asset allocation plan for your goals. That same person will probably be able to suggest suitable investments for each part of the allocation. Once you're comfortable with the financial professional's recommendations, follow the advice and monitor the allocation once or twice a year, as I suggested.

3
How Much Money Do You Need To Retire?

The question I'm asked more than any other is "how much money will I need to retire?" The answer is an individual one, based on your own unique circumstances and desires. The worksheets in this chapter will help you find the right answer for you. (You may want to start with the example that begins on page 35).

Worksheet 1
Retirement Income Calculator

1. Gross income before taxes   _____

2. Multiplier from Table A   _____

3. Multiply item 2 X item 1 = Annual income projected at retirement   _____

4. Choose a multiplier:
   .70 if you're retiring at age 65 or later
   .75 if you're retiring at age 62
   .80 if you're retiring before age 62   _____

5. Multiply item 3 X item 4 = Annual Retirement Income Needed   _____

Ready, Set, Retire!

6. List the assets that you expect will be available at retirement to produce income. Include IRAs, employer-sponsored retirement plans, mutual funds, stocks, bonds, CDs, bank accounts, money market funds, etc. Don't include your residence, autos, boats, etc. that won't produce retirement income for you. **Be realistic** about the amount. Use Worksheet 2 for the future value of current assets. _____

7. Indicate the amount of annual retirement income you expect to be produced by the amount in item 6. A conservative calculation would be item 6 X 5%. A more aggressive estimate would be item 6 X 6% or 7%. _____

8. Show the amount of any known pension plan benefits. Make sure you only include here the benefits that are relatively certain, not those that are based on how much you contribute to the plan in the years between now and retirement. _____

9. Indicate your estimated Social Security benefits. Use Table C for this and add 50% for your spouse's benefits. _____

10. Add the amounts in items 7, 8 and 9. _____

11. Subtract the amount in item 5. (_____)

12. This is the TOTAL _____

How Much Money Do You Need To Retire?

- If item 12 is a positive number, then you should have enough income during retirement.
- If item 12 is a negative number, then you need to do one or more of the following:
  - Increase the benefit levels from Social Security or your employer-sponsored retirement plans.
  - Save more of your income so that you can increase the amount of your assets.
  - Plan to draw on the principal of your savings and investments when you retire.

Worksheet 2 - Assets

Type of Asset	Current Value	Factor From Table B		Future Value
Cash & Savings	_____	X _____	= $	_____
Money-Market Accounts	_____	X _____	= $	_____
Residence	_____	X _____	= $	_____
Company Plans - 1	_____	X _____	= $	_____
Company Plans - 2	_____	X _____	= $	_____
Mutual Funds - 1	_____	X _____	= $	_____
Mutual Funds - 2	_____	X _____	= $	_____
Stocks	_____	X _____	= $	_____
Bonds	_____	X _____	= $	_____
Real Estate	_____	X _____	= $	_____
Limited Partnerships	_____	X _____	= $	_____

Ready, Set, Retire!

Life Insurance - Cash Value - 1 _____ X _____ = $_____

Life Insurance - Cash Value - 2 _____ X _____ = $_____

Collectibles _____ X _____ = $_____

Other _____ X _____ = $_____

TOTAL (A) = $_____

Now list the amount you expect to add to your savings and investments between now and the time you retire. Then do the calculations to determine the future value of these additional investments:

Type of Asset	Annual $ Value You Expect To Add	Factor From Table D	Future Value
_____	_____ X _____		= $_____
_____	_____ X _____		= $_____
_____	_____ X _____		= $_____
	TOTAL (B) = $_____		

FUTURE VALUE OF ASSETS = TOTAL(A) + TOTAL(B) = $_____

Some of these assets won't be subject to tax. But for those that will be taxed, you need to do the following calculations. Multiply the part that is taxed of the Total (A) + Total (B) by 1 minus your tax bracket. E. g. if you're in the 28% tax bracket, 1.00 - .28 = .72. Multiply by .72.

Taxable part of TOTAL(A) + TOTAL(B) from above $_____

Multiply by 1 minus tax bracket (e.g. 1.00 - .28 = .72) _____

After-tax value of taxable part of assets $_____

Non-taxable part of assets $_____

Adjusted TOTAL(A) + TOTAL(B) $_____

Table A - Multiplier For Future Salary

Years Before Retire-ment	% Annual Pay Increase From Now Until Retirement				
	3.0%	4.0%	5.0%	6.0%	7.0%
1	1.030	1.040	1.050	1.060	1.070
2	1.061	1.082	1.103	1.124	1.145
3	1.093	1.125	1.158	1.191	1.225
4	1.126	1.170	1.216	1.263	1.311
5	1.160	1.217	1.276	1.338	1.403
6	1.194	1.265	1.340	1.419	1.501
7	1.230	1.316	1.407	1.504	1.606
8	1.267	1.369	1.478	1.594	1.718
9	1.305	1.423	1.551	1.690	1.839
10	1.344	1.480	1.629	1.791	1.967
12	1.426	1.601	1.796	2.012	2.252
14	1.513	1.732	1.980	2.261	2.579
16	1.605	1.873	2.183	2.540	2.952
18	1.702	2.026	2.407	2.854	3.380
20	1.806	2.191	2.653	3.207	3.870
22	1.916	2.370	2.925	3.604	4.430
24	2.033	2.563	3.225	4.049	5.072
26	2.157	2.773	3.556	4.549	5.807
28	2.288	2.999	3.920	5.112	6.649
30	2.427	3.243	4.322	5.744	7.612
32	2.575	3.508	4.765	6.453	8.715
34	2.732	3.794	5.253	7.251	9.978
36	2.899	4.104	5.792	8.147	11.42
38	3.075	4.439	6.386	9.154	13.08
40	3.262	4.801	7.040	10.29	14.98

Table B - Multiplier For Future Asset Values

Years Before Retirement	Future Value of Investment At Various Rates of Return				
	5.0%	7.0%	9.0%	11.0%	13.0%
1	1.050	1.070	1.090	1.110	1.130
2	1.103	1.145	1.188	1.232	1.277
3	1.158	1.225	1.295	1.368	1.443
4	1.216	1.311	1.412	1.518	1.631
5	1.276	1.403	1.539	1.685	1.842
6	1.340	1.501	1.677	1.870	2.082
7	1.407	1.606	1.828	2.076	2.353
8	1.478	1.718	1.993	2.305	2.658
9	1.551	1.839	2.172	2.558	3.004
10	1.629	1.967	2.367	2.839	3.395
12	1.796	2.252	2.813	3.499	4.335
14	1.980	2.579	3.342	4.310	5.535
16	2.183	2.952	3.970	5.311	7.067
18	2.407	3.380	4.717	6.544	9.024
20	2.653	3.870	5.604	8.062	11.523
22	2.925	4.430	6.659	9.934	14.714
24	3.225	5.072	7.911	12.234	18.788
26	3.556	5.807	9.400	15.080	23.991
28	3.920	6.649	11.167	18.580	30.634
30	3.243	7.612	13.268	22.892	39.116
32	4.765	8.715	15.763	28.206	49.947
34	5.253	9.978	18.728	34.752	63.777
36	5.792	11.424	22.251	42.818	81.437
38	6.386	13.079	26.437	52.756	103.987
40	7.040	14.975	31.409	65.001	132.782

How Much Money Do You Need To Retire?

Table C - Estimated Social Security Benefits

This table assumes that you have had 10 years of earnings under Social Security, and are therefore, fully insured.

Find your estimated Social Security benefit in the columns below. Choose the column that comes closest to matching your earnings as a percentage of the maximum amount on which Social Security taxes are paid. (See Table E for help). For example, if your earnings have averaged 80% of the maximum amount that Social Security taxed, then use the 80% column.

Age At Which You Retire	Earnings As A Percentage Of Social Security Maximum Taxed				
	100%	80%	60%	40%	20%
62	902	866	803	622	451
63	978	939	870	675	489
64	1053	1011	937	726	527
65	1128	1083	1004	778	564

Table D - Multiplier For Added Asset Values

Expected Return	Years To Retirement				
	5	10	15	20	25
4%	5.42	12.01	20.02	29.78	41.65
6%	5.64	13.18	23.28	36.79	54.86
8%	5.87	14.49	27.15	45.76	73.11
10%	6.11	15.94	31.77	57.28	98.35
12%	6.35	17.55	37.28	72.05	133.33

Table E - Social Security Wage Base

These are the maximum amounts on which Social Security taxes were paid.

Year	Wage Base	Year	Wage Base
1951	3,600	1973	10,800
1952	3,600	1974	13,200
1953	3,600	1975	14,100
1954	3,600	1976	15,300
1955	4,200	1977	16,500
1956	4,200	1978	17,700
1957	4,200	1979	22,900
1958	4,200	1980	25,900
1959	4,800	1981	29,700
1960	4,800	1982	32,400
1961	4,800	1983	35,700
1962	4,800	1984	37,800
1963	4,800	1985	39,600
1964	4,800	1986	42,000
1965	4,800	1987	43,800
1966	6,600	1988	45,000
1967	6,600	1989	48,000
1968	7,800	1990	51,300
1969	7,800	1991	53,400
1970	7,800	1992	55,500
1971	7,800	1993	57,600
1972	9,000	1994	60,600

How Much Money Do You Need To Retire?

Let's walk through an example:

Worksheet 1
Retirement Income Calculator

1. Gross income before taxes $ 20,000

2. Multiplier from Table A (e.g. 10 yrs @ 5%)   X 1.629

3. Multiply item 2 X item 1 = Annual
   income projected at retirement $ 32,580

4. Choose a multiplier:
   .70 if you're retiring at age 65 or later
   .75 if you're retiring at age 62
   .80 if you're retiring before age 62
      (e.g. retire at age 62)   .75

5. Multiply item 3 X item 4 = Annual Retirement
   Income Needed   <u>$ 24,435</u>

6. List the assets that you expect will be available
   at retirement to produce income. Include
   IRAs, employer-sponsored retirement plans,
   mutual funds, stocks, bonds, CDs, bank
   accounts, money market funds, etc. Don't
   include your residence, autos, boats, etc.
   that won't produce retirement income for
   you. **Be realistic** about the amount. Use
   Worksheet 2 to calculate the future value
   of assets you have now. $ 96,685

I've given estimates of future rates of return on various assets below. They aren't precise, but you can use them as a starting point for your own calculations in Worksheet 2.

Asset Type	Est. Rate of Return
Cash & Savings	3.0-5.0%
Money-Market Accounts	5.0%
Residence	5.0-7.0%
Stocks	9.0-11.0%
Bonds	5.0-9.0%
Real Estate	5.0-7.0%
Company Plans, Mutual Funds, Limited Partnerships:	Depends on the type of assets in which invested.
Life Insurance	See Policy
Collectibles	Varies

Worksheet 2 - Assets

List the assets you currently have. Then calculate their future values. Looking at Table B, we are using 10 years to retirement. So, for example, Cash & Savings is in the 5% column on the 10 year row = 1.629.

Type of Asset	Current Value		Factor From Table B		Future Value
Cash & Savings	10,000	X	1.629	=	16,290
Money-Market Accounts	5,000	X	1.629	=	8,145

How Much Money Do You Need To Retire?

Residence	0	X	0	=	0
Company Plans - 1	10,757	X	2.367	=	25,462
Company Plans - 2	0	X	0	=	0
Mutual Funds - 1	6,500	X	2.839	=	18,454
Mutual Funds - 2	3,400	X	2.367	=	8,048
Stocks	0	X	0	=	0
Bonds	0	X	0	=	0
Real Estate	12,000	X	1.967	=	23,604
Limited Partnerships	0	X	0	=	0
Life Insurance-Cash Value-1	0	X	0	=	0
Life Insurance-Cash Value-2	0	X	0	=	0
Collectibles	0	X	0	=	0
Other	0	X	0	=	0
	TOTAL (A)			=	100,003

Now list the amount you expect to add to your savings and investments between now and the time you retire. Then do the calculations to determine the future value of these additional investments.

Type of Asset	Annual $ Value You Expect To Add		Factor From Table D		Future Value
Mutual Fund-Growth	2,000	X	15.94	=	31,880
Bank Savings	200	X	12.01	=	2,402
			TOTAL (B)	=	34,282
Future Value Of Assets = TOTAL(A) + TOTAL(B)				=	134,285

Some of the assets you've included here won't be subject to tax. For those things that will be taxed, however, you need to do the following calculations. Multiply the taxable parts of the Total (A) + Total (B) by 1 minus your tax bracket. E. g. if you're in the 28% tax bracket, 1-.28=.72. Multiply by .72.

Taxable part of TOTAL(A)+TOTAL(B) (This includes everything except items that won't be taxed, e.g. municipal bonds, tax-free loans from insurance policies, etc. Here, there are no such items, so everything is taxable.)	134,285
Multiply by 1-tax bracket	.72
After-tax value of taxable part of assets	96,685
Non-taxable part of assets	0
Adjusted TOTAL(A) + TOTAL(B)	96,685

How Much Money Do You Need To Retire?

7. Indicate the amount of annual retirement
    income you expect to be produced by the
    amount in item 6. A conservative
    calculation would be item 6 X 5%.
    A more aggressive estimate would be
    item 6 X 6% or 7%. (e.g. use 7%)   6,798

8. Show the amount of any known pension plan
    benefits. Make sure you only include here
    the benefits that are relatively certain,
    not those that are based on how much you
    contribute to the plan in the years
    between now and retirement. Here, we'll
    assume there's no pension plan benefit.   0

9. Indicate your estimated Social Security
    benefits. Use Table C for this and add
    50% for your spouse's benefits. Here,
    assume that lifetime earnings averaged 80%
    of the maximum amount that Social Security
    taxed. Also, assume retirement begins at
    age 62 and that there's no spouse.   866

10. Add the amounts in items 7, 8 and 9. This
    is the total income that will be provided
    by assets, pensions and Social Security.   7,664

11. Subtract the amount in item 5. This is the
    annual retirement income needed.   (24,435)

12. This is the TOTAL. (If this is positive, it
    represents excess income; if negative, it
    represents a shortage of income.)   (16,770)

Since item 12 is a negative number (i.e. item 11 is larger than item 10), this person will need to do one or more of the following:

- Increase the benefit levels from Social Security or employer-sponsored retirement plans.

- Save a larger amount of income to increase the amount of assets.

- Plan to draw on the principal of his or her savings and investments for retirement income.

Now you know! Do you need more assets? If you do, you're like most people.

The next chapter will show you that income taxes are a major consideration in getting you from where you are today to where you want to be by the time you retire. Tax considerations will also let you stretch a limited nest egg over many more years of retirement.

4
Taxes! Taxes! Taxes!

Do you feel the IRS nipping at your heals? Are you paying your *fair share*, whatever that is? Most people feel their tax bite is too large. Tax rates of 28% and 31% are now standard for most people. That's after you've already paid 7.65% of your income (up to $60,600 in 1994) for Social Security and Medicare taxes. Your employer paid a matching 7.65% of your income on top of that.

Then there's a state income tax in most states. There are city and other local income taxes. Gasoline taxes may make you fume. If you puff or imbibe, you'll pay taxes. Do you use beauty aids? More taxes. Do you own a dog or cat? They'll cost you taxes. Everywhere you look, there's something that's taxed. In fact, the average American now works more than four months of every year just to pay taxes.

Is all this tax talk taxing your patience? Well, although it may not be possible to just say "Enough is enough!" there *are* things most of us can do about it.

The Two Kinds of Income Tax Returns

Which Kind Are You Using?

Did you know that there are two kinds of federal income tax returns? Well it may not be true, technically. But it is abundantly clear that *something* more than assets and incomes separates the paupers from the billionaires, when it comes to income taxes. That *something* is *information*. *Being informed* about taxes makes the difference.

Consider the tax return of a person with very little information about how to save on taxes. It might look something like this:

Uninformed Income Tax Return

Income earned from work	$	50,000
Income earned from savings		
and investments		2,000
Gross Income	$	52,000
Deductions:		
Real estate taxes	$	2,250
Income taxes - state & local		2,860
Home mortgage interest		7,000
Charitable contributions		300

Personal exemptions - self, spouse, and two children		9,400
Total Deductions	$	21,810
Taxable Income	$	30,190
Federal Income Tax	$	4,529
+State/Local Income Tax		2,860
Total Tax	$	7,389

Compare this to an *informed* taxpayer's return:

Informed
Income Tax Return

Income earned from work	$	50,000
Income earned from savings and investments		2,000
Gross Income	$	52,000
Deductions from Income:		
Tax-deferred income		*900*
Tax-free income		*300*
Income not reportable		*600*
Adjusted Gross Income	$	50,200

Deductions:

Real estate taxes	$	2,250
Income taxes - state & local		2,761
Home mortgage interest		7,000
Charitable contributions		300
Personal exemptions - self, spouse, and two children		9,400
Total Deductions	$	21,711
Taxable Income	$	28,489
Preliminary Federal Income Tax	$	4,273

Deductions from Tax to be Paid:
Tax credits

Tax credits		*1,500*
Federal Income Tax	$	2,773
+State/Local Income Tax		2,761
Total Tax	$	5,534
Difference in Taxes Paid	**$**	**1,855**
% SAVINGS		**25.1%**

If you're not yet retired, I'm sure you want to reach your retirement goals. If you're already retired, I'm also sure you'd like to live a more prosperous life. To achieve either of these, it's clear that you need to reduce the effect of taxes on your investments.

The next several chapters will focus on those clever **_Deductions_** you probably noted on the **_Informed_** Tax Return that were missing from the **_Uninformed_** Tax Return. But first, here's a summary of those deductions for *your **Informed*** tax return:

Deductions From Income:

Tax-deferred income

- Individual Retirement Accounts (IRAs)
- 401(k), 403(b), Keogh and SEP Retirement Plans
- Private Pensions
- Nonqualified Salary Deferral Plans
- Tax-Deferred Annuities — Immediate, Fixed and Variable
- Capital Gains
- Series EE U.S. Government Bonds
- Cash Value Build-up Life Insurance Policies
- Universal Life Insurance Policies

Tax-free income

- Private Pensions
- Nonqualified Salary Deferral Plans
- Capital Gains, When Held Until Death
- Series EE U. S. Government Bonds — When Used To Pay College Tuition & Fees
- Cash Value Build-Up Life Insurance Policies
- Universal Life Insurance Policies
- Municipal Bonds — Same State as Residence
- Municipal Bonds — NOT Same State as Residence
- Municipal Bond Unit Investment Trusts — Insured and Non-Insured; Same State as Residence or National
- Municipal Bond Mutual Funds — Same State as Residence or National

Income Not Reportable

- Individual Retirement Accounts (IRAs)
- 401(k), 403(b), Keogh and SEP Retirement Plans
- Private Pensions
- Nonqualified Salary Deferral Plans
- Tax-Deferred Annuities — Fixed and Variable
- Capital Gains, Not Reportable Until Realized
- Series EE U.S. Government Bonds, If You Choose
- Cash Value Build-Up Life Insurance Policies

- Universal Life Insurance Policies

Deductions From Tax To Be Paid:

Tax Credits

- Foreign Tax Credit
- Historic Structure Rehabilitation Credit
- Affordable Housing Tax Credit

I'll devote a separate chapter to each of these deductions. Please keep in mind that this is not intended to be a comprehensive list of things you can do to reduce the sting of taxes on your plans for retirement. And some of the items may not be appropriate for your situation. The items discussed, however, are what I believe to be those having the most universal appeal — and ones that are often overlooked.

In the upcoming chapters on specific tax deductions, I've indicated a series of ratings for each deduction. What follows is a discussion of those ratings.

(I strongly suggest that you consult a tax professional and a financial professional before investing your money in any of the items described in this book.)

*The government wastes so much money
it might as well give away
free samples of the stuff.*
— *Anon.*

5
Ratings Of Deductions

Ratings are a shorthand way to quickly flip through a list of choices. Whether you're looking for a good movie or a good motel, a rating can help you eliminate ones in which you don't have an interest. Investment choices are no different. The ratings I've used are, admittedly, unscientific. They're based on my own personal opinion, and they may not apply to your individual financial situation. But in the words of that great investment counselor and singing nun, Julie Andrews, "I have confidence in me!" And what the heck, you have to start somewhere, don't you?! So, I've rated each investment type discussed for things that I've found to be important to investors. Ratings are represented by smiles. 5 smiles (☺☺☺☺☺) is the highest rating for the indicated characteristic and 1 smile (☺) is the lowest. Kind of makes you feel warm all over, doesn't it?

1. Comfort
This one is easy. This rating is based on the answer to the question "how well will I sleep at night if my money is invested in this way?" If you

don't understand the investment, it shouldn't get a 5-smile (☺ ☺ ☺ ☺ ☺) rating for comfort. Similarly, a person who has consistently lost money in the stock market would be wise to give stock market investments only 1 or 2 smiles for comfort.

Why is comfort important? I've found over the years that investors who aren't comfortable with an investment are likely to unload it at the worst possible time — just to be rid of it. The *dis*comfort just gets too great. They become irritable and start to lose sleep. Besides, I've found most people don't want to worry about their money, they want to enjoy it.

2. <u>Convenience</u>

I'm often reminded of the story about a fellow in New York City who wanted to do something nice for his fellow man. He felt he had far more money than he needed. So he decided to give some of it away. Every day, for about a week, he stood on a busy street corner and gave away $1 bills to everyone who passed by.

Now you might expect that this fellow would be mobbed by people looking for the free money. In fact, quite the opposite happened. Many people who passed near this corner simply didn't want to bother with going across the street, or fighting the crowds, or waiting in line — all for $1. It just wasn't *convenient!*

Your time is worth something, obviously. If an investment uses up too much of it, you'll be unlikely to use it and enjoy its rewards. So I've included a rating to describe how easy or difficult it is to make the investment and to monitor its progress over time.

3. Income and Appreciation

This one is a bit more complicated, but not too difficult. An investment that spits out cash like a slot machine hitting the jackpot clearly deserves a 5-smile (☺ ☺ ☺ ☺ ☺) rating for Income and Appreciation. Heck, you'd have to be a pretty dull person if an investment like that didn't put a few smiles on your face. One that only earns a low rate of interest and no capital appreciation, however, would only get a 1-smile (☺) rating. Please note, however, that I'm talking about the *potential* for income and capital appreciation, based on its history. So an investment that has a 5-smile (☺ ☺ ☺ ☺ ☺) rating for income and appreciation has a history of excellent income and/or appreciation. But there is no assurance the future will be as good or even that it will be positive. Unfortunately, only death and taxes are guaranteed, but I'm working hard here to chip away at that second one. Which brings us to...

4. Tax Savings

Does the investment save a lot of taxes? If the answer is a Big Yes, then it deserves a 5-smile (☺ ☺ ☺ ☺ ☺) rating for Tax Savings. The question here is "how many dollars in taxes are saved in relation to the dollars invested?" The greater the tax savings per dollar invested, the higher the rating.

Try to avoid a mistake I've seen many people make over the years. In their relentless pursuit of tax-savings, some people invest their money in things that have very little economic value. In the end, they may save some money in taxes. But they also lose the money they've invested. That's the sad result of over-emphasizing the importance of tax-savings.

5. Sex Appeal

Come on now, let's face it. Some investments are just a lot more fun than others. How excited can you get about a passbook savings account? Sure, the teller at the bank may stir some primordial juices as he or she processes your deposit slip. But does the savings account itself cause any stirring in your loins?

Be honest, wouldn't you rather own a Picasso than a plot of desert land in west Texas? But then, how would you feel if beneath that Texas sagebrush there was a ten million barrel pool of oil?

To have Sex Appeal, an investment must be interesting to the investor. Since most investors are likely to hold onto investments with sex appeal longer than ones without it, it might be appropriate to invest where your interests lie.

Be careful, though. Don't invest in something simply because it is interesting. Don't let the dazzling sex appeal blind you to the economic flaws of an investment. I've seen an awful lot of investments sparkle their way into major disappointments or bankruptcy.

I remember, for example, that the stocks of condom manufacturers skyrocketed when AIDS awareness first began to take hold. It seemed not to matter that condoms didn't really account for much of any individual company's earnings. The stocks just kept rising, anyway. (If you see a pun here, congratulations! It's a sure sign that you still have a pulse.)

As the price of one company's stock rose from 60 to 130, its management said this was crazy.

Condoms weren't that profitable, they said, and accounted for less than a third of the company's sales. Still, the fervor drove the stock to over 150 before sanity returned. When it did, though, the stock retraced its gain all the way back to the low 60s. Unfortunately, there probably weren't many who escaped during the rapid price slide. Safe sex? Not in this case.

6
Tax Deductions YOU Can Use

6.A.
Good Things Come
In Small Packages

Individual Retirement Accounts (IRAs)

Ratings

If invested in stocks, stock mutual funds, or other equity type investments:

Comfort	☺ ☺ ☺
Convenience	☺ ☺ ☺ ☺
Income & Appreciation	☺ ☺ ☺ ☺ ☺
Tax Savings	☺ ☺ ☺ ☺
Sex Appeal	☺

If invested in low return, guaranteed fixed income type investments:

Comfort	☺ ☺ ☺ ☺ ☺
Convenience	☺ ☺ ☺ ☺
Income & Appreciation	☺
Tax Savings	☺ ☺ ☺ ☺
Sex Appeal	☺

If you earn money, you can have an Individual Retirement Account (IRA). If you earn money and don't have an IRA, you're missing one of the best tax-smart investments around.

Like geese flying north for summer, people used to flock to banks and brokerage offices every April to make their IRA contributions. Then the Revenue Hunters in Congress took aim at the tax deduction for IRA contributions for many taxpayers. Overnight, IRA contributors were reduced from enormous flocks to an endangered species.

Prior to the rule change, most people who contributed to their IRAs did so to take advantage of the tax deduction their contribution provided. They could subtract the amount of their IRA contribution right off their earned income for the year and thus avoid paying taxes on that amount. Their tax return preparers told them that they could either put $2,000 in their IRA or they'd have to send Uncle Sam another $560 in non-refundable taxes (assuming a 28% tax bracket). That was a pretty simple choice for most people. When the rules changed to eliminate the immediate tax deduction for many people, however, most of these people simply saw no advantage in making further contributions. Too bad!

As I'll explain, it is the tax *deferral, not* the *tax deduction* that makes an IRA such a powerful tax-smart investment.

Let's look at the basics. An IRA is a plan that allows a taxpayer to accumulate retirement money tax-deferred, i.e. you don't pay taxes on the accumulated earnings until the money is withdrawn. With certain limitations, the individual taxpayer decides how to invest the money.

You can invest up to $2,000 of earned income each year (or $2,250 if you also contribute to an IRA for a non-working spouse). If you're a member of the Put-It-Off-Till-Tomorrow Club, you'll also like the fact that you have until April 15th of the following year to make your contribution.

Your IRA contribution may or may not be deductible, depending on your circumstances. For example, you can deduct **all** of your IRA contribution if:

- you are not covered by a retirement plan where you work

  - OR -

- you are single and have adjusted gross income of less than $25,000 a year

  - OR -

- you are married and earn less than $40,000 a year.

You may be eligible for a **partial** IRA deduction if you have adjusted gross income between $25,000 and $35,000 (single) or between $40,000 and $50,000 (married filing jointly).

Although many people don't realize it, you can still make an IRA contribution even if you don't qualify for a tax deduction.

Should you make such non-deductible contributions? I think the answer is usually YES! Since your money will grow untouched by taxes inside your IRA, it will compound much faster than it would in a taxable investment outside of your IRA. Outside of your IRA, you'll have to pay taxes each year on the money your investment earns.

Let's look at an example of how money can grow inside and outside of an IRA:

You invest $2,000 per year.
You make your investments each year for 30 years.
You earn an annual compound growth rate of 10% (That's what the Standard & Poor's 500 Composite Index has averaged over the past 25 years).

The table below shows how the money would have grown for a taxable investment, a deductible IRA and a non-deductible IRA.

Final Value of Investment
After Withdrawing the Money & Paying Taxes

Tax Bracket	Taxable Investment	Deductible IRA	Non-Deductible IRA
28%	$152,611	$261,974	$200,688
36%	$116,842	$232,866	$162,830

(See Appendix A for details)

Even if your IRA contribution isn't tax deductible, the *deferral* of tax on the growth will enable the non-deductible IRA to grow $48,077 ($200,688 - $152,611 = $48,077) or 32% more than a taxable investment for a 28% tax bracket taxpayer. Similarly, a non-deductible IRA will grow $45,988 ($162,830 - $116,842 = $45,988) or 39% more than a taxable investment for a 36% tax bracket taxpayer. Those are pretty compelling numbers!

So, you've decided to make IRA contributions. What do you invest in? I think you need to invest in things that will give you broad diversification (for safety) and an opportunity for an above-average rate of return. Mutual funds that invest in common stocks seem to fill the bill nicely, in my opinion.

Other investment advisors may suggest investments that have historically produced much lower rates of return, like Treasury Bills and long-term bonds. With the combination of broad diversification and a long-term time frame, however, I think the greater volatility of common stock mutual funds should smooth out and produce a far better retirement nest egg.

The differences in return between these investments have been *huge*. There have been numerous studies that show the same results — over the last 65+ years, stocks have outperformed long-term government bonds by 30 to 1 and short-term government securities by 63 to 1. For increased purchasing power, Treasuries and long-term bonds just haven't matched common stocks in the long run.

Rollovers

I'm often asked to comment on rolling over employer retirement plan assets into an IRA. Although I don't think this book is the place for a recitation of all the detailed rules, I do want to make you aware of a potential trap. Under Internal Revenue Code Section 402, there's a mandatory 20% federal income tax withholding on funds paid *directly* to plan participants. To avoid paying the tax, both the funds distributed **AND** the amount withheld must be rolled over into an

IRA.

That's the trap. You can't roll over the withheld portion if you don't get your hands on it. So wham, you can end up paying income tax and the 10% premature withdrawal penalty on the amount that's withheld — all because the funds were paid directly to you, and you couldn't get your hands on the 20% that was withheld.

To avoid this trap, have the employer retirement plan assets moved *directly* into an IRA without ever coming into your hands. Since employers are required to offer this direct rollover option, you shouldn't ever be forced into the trap. I don't call them Congressional Revenue Hunters for nothing, so watch out!

Premature Withdrawals

Please note that withdrawals from an IRA prior to reaching 59½ are also generally subject to income tax *and a 10% penalty.* So you probably shouldn't contribute money to an IRA that you know you'll need before you turn 59½.

Other Cautions

Also note that you can't borrow money from an IRA, you can't use an IRA as security for a loan, and you can't sell property to an IRA. But you probably *can* live happily ever after if you make annual contributions and invest those contributions wisely.

Required Distributions

Are you ever *required* to take money out of your IRA? Only if you want to avoid a whopping 50% penalty on excess accumulations when the required annual minimum distribution isn't made.

Do I have your attention? Good! Now please turn down the background music and read the following carefully — this is going to get a little complicated.

To avoid the 50% penalty, you have to begin taking money out of your IRA no later than April 1 of the year following the calendar year in which you turn 70½. Thereafter, there's a required distribution each year that must be made by December 31 of each year.

Let's look at an example. If you were born on January 1, 1930, you'd turn 70 on January 1, 2000. And, on July 1, 2000, you'd be 70½. So you'd turn 70½ in the calendar year of 2000. You must begin distributions from your IRA no later than April 1, 2001, i.e. the year following the calendar year in which you turn 70½. Then you'd also have to make *another* distribution by December 31, 2001. You'd have to make still another distribution every year thereafter by December 31 of each year.

Some people have made contributions to IRA accounts at a variety of institutions over the years. The amount that you're required to take out each year is based on the balance in all of your IRA accounts at the beginning of the year. The actual distribution can come from any, all, or only one of your IRAs, however you choose.

You can take money out of your IRAs in a lump-sum or in the form of periodic distributions that will take the account value to zero over your life expectancy. If you choose the periodic method, and it is probably to your advantage to do so, special life expectancy tables are used to calculate the required minimum distribution each year. I think you'd be wise to consult a tax professional to help you with these calculations. Remember, a *50% penalty* awaits those who make a mistake.

6.B.
Alphabet Soup
To Warm Your Retirement

401(k), 403(b), Keogh (HR10) and SEP

Ratings

If invested in stocks, stock mutual funds, or other equity type investments:

Comfort		☺ ☺ ☺
Convenience:	*Keogh*	☺
	Other Types	☺ ☺ ☺ ☺
Income & Appreciation		☺ ☺ ☺ ☺ ☺
Tax Savings		☺ ☺ ☺ ☺
Sex Appeal		☺ ☺ ☺ ☺

If invested in low return, guaranteed fixed income type investments:

Comfort		☺ ☺ ☺ ☺ ☺
Convenience:	*Keogh*	☺
	Other Types	☺ ☺ ☺ ☺
Income & Appreciation		☺
Tax Savings		☺ ☺ ☺ ☺
Sex Appeal		☺ ☺ ☺ ☺

401(k)

The 401(k) Plan is a type of retirement plan offered by an increasing number of employers. Under this plan, you can deduct a percentage of your pre-tax salary and have it invested in a tax-deferred retirement account. You get two benefits. First, you get a deduction from your taxable income. Second, the money in the plan will accumulate tax-deferred until you withdraw it during your retirement years. So far, so good.

What makes 401(k) plans so popular, however, is that most companies offer to match at least a portion of your contribution. Suppose your employer has a 401(k) plan and offers to contribute 50 cents for each dollar that you put into the plan. Suppose, also, that your employer's generosity will run out when you've contributed 6% of your salary. So for every $100 you put in up to 6% of your salary, your employer will put in $50. How can you beat that?! That's a 50% rate of return on your money — with no risk!

What's amazing to me is that a quarter of all the people who are eligible for such plans fail to participate. Especially when the employer matches a part of the employee's contribution, I can't think of a better retirement program.

Some people complain that they can't afford to lock

up their money until retirement. Maybe so, but I'd simply ask them where they're going to get a better deal. When their employer matches their contribution, it's free money. I'd also point out that most 401(k) plans allow employees to borrow from the plan if they really need the money.

For people looking to sock away more than an IRA will allow, the 401(k) is also ideal. For 1994, an employee can make an annual contribution up to $9,240, or 15% of wages, whichever is less. This amount is adjusted each year for inflation. It gets even better if the employer matches all or a part of the employee's contribution. Then the combined contribution is generally limited to 15% of wages, up to a maximum contribution of $30,000.

Call me a worrywart or a cynic if you want. I'm just worried that those Revenue Hunters in Congress will discover what a good deal 401(k) plans really are. People are pouring billions of tax deductible dollars into these plans, and the money will stay there, tax-deferred, for years to come. 401(k) plans will sooner or later attract more Congressional attention. I'll dash to my TV and tune in the weather channel to see if, in fact, hell really has frozen over if Congress ever stops trying to come up with new ways to raise revenue. So I urge people to take advantage of their 401(k) opportunities while they last.

How should you invest the money that's in your 401(k)? Far too many people, I think, treat this decision with the same importance as other company lunch-room topics of conversation:

Chris: "Say, Marty. What are you doin' with your 401(k) money?"

Marty: "I dunno. Half in the bond fund, I think. And the other half in some kinda stock thing."

Chris: "Yeah. That sounds pretty good."
          "Who do ya think'll win the game to-night?"

Until recently, most 401(k) plan participants have been left to their own devices, however meager, to decipher their plan options. Companies with 401(k) plans frequently haven't offered their employees much help in understanding how the plan works or how to make appropriate investment choices.

Recent federal regulations have changed that. The regulations, called 404(c), encourage employers to give their employees more information about making investment decisions, more investment choices from which to choose, and the ability to switch their money among the choices. Although companies don't have to comply with the 404(c) regulations, compliance will certainly reduce the company's potential legal liability. Or would it be too much to expect Congress to require compliance, thereby giving people the same level of protection they give feathered tree turtles and spotted owls?

If you are eligible to participate in a 401(k), I strongly encourage you to ask your employer for thorough information about your plan. You need to spend more than a few moments in the lunch-room gathering and examining the information. After all, the 401(k) plan money is potentially the largest single piece of your retirement program. It deserves your serious and complete attention.

If your plan allows you to invest in a fund that seeks long-term growth, I think you ought to consider putting most of your money there. Over time, growth-oriented investments have provided a much better hedge against inflation than income-oriented investments. Day-to-day fluctuations shouldn't be of much concern since the long-term nature of the investment should help to smooth them out.

There are two investments I think you probably should avoid, however. The first one is the "guaranteed" account. This may be called by another name in your plan, perhaps "fixed income" or "fixed rate." As

I've said to you earlier, what is *guaranteed* is that the investment will usually lose purchasing power. Instead, I think you probably should invest in the growth-oriented options your plan has available.

The second investment I'd generally avoid is the stock of your own company. Some 401(k) plans allow you to invest in the stock of your company. Although you may work for a very fine company, I'd ask whether you thought you had enough of your eggs in your company's basket already. I saw a lot of unhappy IBM employees go through the anguish of getting laid off just at the time their investments in IBM were dropping to new lows. Could that happen to you? Think about it.

I should add a note of caution before I end this discussion of 401(k) plans. Not long ago, a fellow I know on the West Coast borrowed $10,000 from his 401(k) plan for part of the down payment on a new house. Six months later, he was laid off from his job. He found another job a month later, so his lost income from being laid off was not a major problem.

But then his former employer told him that since he was no longer their employee, they'd have to distribute his 401(k) money to him. At first, he didn't think that was a problem, since he could roll over the money into an IRA to avoid the tax and premature withdrawal penalty.

Then the roof fell in. His former employer told him that if he didn't repay the $10,000 401(k) plan loan, they would have to report it as a premature distribution from the plan. Since he didn't have the money available, he had no choice but to accept it that way. Ouch!

As a premature distribution, the $10,000 became fully taxable for income tax purposes. In his tax bracket, that cost him $2,800. On top of that, the $10,000 became subject to the 10% penalty on a premature distribution. Bang, another $1,000. So here he was, out of a job for a month, and now facing taxes and penalties totaling $3,800 — all because he'd borrowed from his 401(k) plan and then couldn't repay the loan.

My advice, then, is to be careful about borrowing from a 401(k) plan. Such borrowing should only be for true emergencies and, preferably, in small amounts.

403(b)

The 403(b) Tax-Sheltered Annuity (TSA) is very similar to the 401(k), but with some differences. A TSA participant must be an employee of a tax-exempt charitable, educational, or religious organization, or the Department of Defense. (Don't ask. I would have loved to have been a fly on the wall in the Congressional back office when the military got added!) This program includes teachers, hospital employees and many others.

Like the 401(k), a person looking for a way to go beyond the low contribution limits of an IRA will find the 403(b) attractive. An employee can make an annual contribution up to 20% of earned income, times the years of service, minus the tax-free contributions made in prior years. This contribution is limited to $9,500 (for 1993). If the employer matches all or part of the employee's contribution, the combined contribution is generally limited to 25% of wages, up to a maximum contribution of $30,000. There are special rules that allow some employees to qualify for extra contributions above these limits.

If you're an employee of a school, church, hospital, health and welfare agency or any qualifying organization that offers a 403(b), you should seriously consider contributing to the plan. I also urge you to follow the investment suggestions given for the 401(k) plan.

Keogh (HR10)

Only partnerships and sole proprietorships can set up a Keogh plan. Congress really outdid itself on this one. Keogh plans are probably the most complicated of any plan an individual could use. But I won't dwell here on the detailed rules that apply to them.

Even with the complications, however, you should consider a Keogh in some circumstances. If you're self-employed, make a lot of money and want to put a bunch of it away for retirement, a Keogh may be a good bet. The Defined Benefit Keogh will allow you to put away either 100% of your average net income during your three highest income years or $115,641 (for 1993), whichever is less. This is a great program for those who want to put away a lot of money and have the money to do it.

You should seek the advice of a tax professional prior to establishing such a plan.

SEP

A Simplified Employee Pension (SEP) is an IRA or a group of IRAs. Your employer contributes to the IRAs on behalf of its employees.

Once the employer's contribution is made, the money in the IRA is treated the same as any other IRA money.

Why do employer's like them? Simplicity! Unlike 401(k), 403(b) and Keogh plans, there is very little paperwork. There are generally no annual reporting requirements for SEPs. If you're self-employed and have been through the hassle of filing a Form 5500, you'll understand and appreciate the simplicity of a SEP.

The contribution limit for a self-employed person using a SEP is 13.0435% of compensation, up to a maximum contribution of $30,000. (I guess the simplicity of a SEP plan is relative. Compared to a Keogh, a SEP is simple. Compared to something written by someone outside of Congress, a SEP is not simple.) An employee participating in a SEP is allowed a contribution of 15% of wages up to $30,000.

Why might an employer not like a SEP? Well, consider George Greenthumb. George runs a small nursery. During the summer, when his business is blooming, he hires a few extra employees. Then when the fall winds blow away his customers, he lays these employees off. Most of them work for him only one season.

If George has a SEP and makes contributions for any employees, the rules generally require him to make contributions for everyone who worked for him during the year. He must contribute to the IRA of people who no longer work for him and probably never will again. Like many employers, George doesn't want to make contributions like that, and probably won't want a SEP.

The rules governing 401(k), 403(b), Keogh and SEP

plans are rather complicated and too lengthy to include here. I suggest that employees who can participate in 401(k) or 403(b) plans should consult their organization's employee benefits office to become familiar with the features of their plan. If you're considering a Keogh or SEP plan, I urge you to consult a tax professional for more details.

Ready, Set, Retire!

6.C.
Cut The Red Tape

Private Pensions

<u>Ratings</u>

Comfort	☺ ☺ ☺ ☺ ☺
Convenience	☺ ☺ ☺
Income & Appreciation	☺ ☺ ☺ ☺ ☺
Tax Savings	☺ ☺ ☺ ☺ ☺
Sex Appeal	☺ ☺ ☺ ☺ ☺

How would you like to turn $108,000 into $1,050,000 — *tax-free?* Would you also like to do it without going through a lot of governmental red tape? Well, it can be done through what is known as a Private Pension Plan (PPP). Let's start with an example.

Jack Overtaxed is 35 years old. For the next 30 years, until he's 65 years old, he'd like to invest $3,600 per year toward his retirement.

His friend, Pat Planahead, is a creative insurance agent with a highly rated insurance company. Pat

Planahead suggests that Jack consider a Private Pension Plan. "The Private Pension Plan," Pat explains, "will convert your after-tax dollars into a retirement income stream that's tax-free."

"How's that?" Jack asks.

"First," says Pat, "you put your $3,600 per year into an account with my insurance company. For the next 30 years my company will keep your money and invest it for you."

"OK," Jack says. "But what about that tax-free retirement income?"

"I'm just coming to that," Pat says. "When you turn 65, Jack, you will begin to receive an income stream of $35,000 per year."

"$35,000 per year?" Jack asks in disbelief. "That's almost 10 times what I invested per year!"

"That's true," Pat says. "But that's not the best part."

"No?" Jack asks.

"No! The best part is that the $35,000 per year is tax-free."

"What's the catch?" Jack asks. "How long does this tax-free $35,000 per year last?"

"You're not going to believe it," Pat says confidently. "It will last for 30 years. The same number of years that you invested your $3,600 per year."

"So I get $35,000 for 30 years? Tax free? Until

I'm 95?" Jack asks awestruck. Jack's fingers fly over the buttons on his pocket calculator. "Why that's $1,050,000! And I only invested $108,000!"

"That's right," Pat says proudly. "But there's more!"

"More?"

"Yes," Pat begins. "As good as this Private Pension Plan is, there's the problem that you may not live long enough to enjoy it."

"True," Jack says glumly.

Pat leans back casually and smiles a wide, toothy grin. "If you slam into a rock parasailing before you reach retirement, Jack, my company will give your wife Susie and your kids a check for $100,000."

"Hey, I don't do that crazy parasailing any more," Jack says. "I guess I'm getting chicken."

"Chicken! I'd say you're getting smart," Pat says. "Regardless, if for any reason you don't make it to retirement, Susie and the kids will get the money."

"But I don't need any more life insurance," Jack complains. "You already sold me enough of that last year."

"True, again," Pat says. "Try not to think of this as a life insurance policy."

"But that's what it is."

"Yes, it is. But what we're really doing here is using the advantages of a life insurance policy to fund a retirement plan that you control."

"I don't understand," Jack says.

"Look," Pat explains. "The cash value in a life insurance policy is allowed to grow without paying any income tax on the increase in value. It's tax-deferred."

"OK, I'm with you so far."

"When it comes time for you to retire," Pat continues, "you can take that cash out of the policy and use it for retirement income."

"But how is it tax-free?" Jack asks.

"Because you're merely borrowing it from the policy. And you don't pay tax on the money you get in a loan."

"Pretty slick, Pat!" Jack says. "Where do I sign?"

So far, so good. But there are some important considerations before *you* sign up for such a plan. First, you should understand that this is a **non**-qualified pension plan arrangement. As such, the money you put into it is not tax-deductible. Second, you should understand that a Universal Life Insurance Policy is usually the vehicle used for a Private Pension Plan. As an insurance policy, you should remember that:

- A greater portion of your investment will go toward paying a death benefit if you are older than if you are younger. Therefore, less will go toward building the cash value that you'll be able to use for retirement income. In general, someone in reasonably good health and not over 55 may find these arrangements useful.

- As with all insurance policies, the financial strength of the company issuing the policy is important. (See the section on Tax-Deferred Annuities in Chapter 6.E. for a discussion of insurance company safety.)

A critical feature of the Private Pension Plan (PPP) is your cost of borrowing from the insurance policy. A policy that charges a high interest rate on the loans will make it less desirable as a vehicle for the PPP.

Insurance policies generally charge the owner for borrowing from the policy. At the same time, most policies credit back to the policy's cash value a certain amount of interest on the loaned funds. The difference in the interest charged and the interest credited is called the *net interest charge.*

As the table on the next page shows, even a *small* net interest charge for the policy loans will make a *big* difference in the amount of income the policy will provide. To make sure you get the best deal, ask about the net interest charge before you invest. It should be as close to zero as possible.

Interest Charged On Loaned Funds	Interest Credited On Loaned Funds		Net Interest Charge	Percent Of Available Income Lost As Loan Rate Increases
4.0%	— 4.0%	=	0.0%	0.0%
4.5%	— 4.0%	=	0.5%	5.5%
5.0%	— 4.0%	=	1.0%	9.0%
5.5%	— 4.0%	=	1.5%	13.3%
6.0%	— 4.0%	=	2.0%	17.4%

There are also some things to consider that are unique to the type of universal life insurance policy used. First, there's the kind that will credit a *fixed* rate of interest to the cash value each month, quarter, year, etc. Since the rate is subject to change, it's wise to inquire about the company's history of interest rate renewals. How good has the company been about keeping its interest rates in line with the rates generally available in the market place?

There's another kind of policy called a *Variable* Universal Life Insurance Policy. The rate of return you earn will fluctuate, and will depend on the investment performance of the various subaccounts within the policy. A Variable Universal Life Insurance Policy is, in essence, a family of mutual funds all wrapped up in a life insurance policy package. The advantage is that you can get the growth potential of mutual funds combined with the tax-deferred growth and tax-free income benefits of an insurance policy. For a complete discussion of Variable Universal Life Insurance, see Chapter 6.J. — The Jackpot.

There's an important risk I should mention here. Insurance agents are permitted to give you an illustration of how an insurance policy will perform. These illustrations generally show how the policy's cash value will increase, how loans can be taken out of that cash value, and the death benefit that will be payable at certain ages over the life of the policy.

The problem is that these are merely projections. They're estimates of what will happen in the future. Too often, I think, a potential policy owner is subjected to what I call the Fantastic Forecast Risk. How likely is it that you'll be able to achieve a 12% rate of return on your investment in a Universal Life policy? Insurance agents are usually allowed to show you a projection using that 12% rate.

If the Fantastic Forecast comes true, great! If it doesn't, however, the policy owner is likely to be very surprised and disappointed. To make it worse, that disappointment may not occur until many years later when the policy owner is too old to do much about it.

So be cautious. Most insurance agents will be more than happy to provide you with illustrations based on whatever rate of return assumption you desire. I'd suggest you look at illustrations using rates of return in the 7-10% area. If you've followed the *Five Steps For Comfortable Investing*, and invested in a diversified portfolio of subaccounts that emphasize growth, a 7-10% rate of return should be realistic over the long-term.

6.D.
"Trust Me" Plans

"Nonqualified" Salary Deferral Plans

Ratings
If plan is <u>NOT</u> funded with an insurance policy:

Comfort	☺
Convenience	☺ ☺ ☺ ☺
Income & Appreciation	☺ ☺ ☺
Tax Savings	☺ ☺ ☺ ☺
Sex Appeal	☺ ☺ ☺ ☺ ☺

If plan <u>IS</u> funded with an insurance policy:

Comfort	☺ ☺ ☺ ☺
Convenience	☺ ☺
Income & Appreciation	☺ ☺ ☺ ☺
Tax Savings	☺ ☺ ☺ ☺
Sex Appeal	☺ ☺ ☺ ☺ ☺

These plans are clearly NOT for everyone. There are NO guarantees of any kind with this kind of plan. The employer merely *promises* to pay the employee an amount of money in the future.

Since the plan doesn't qualify for special tax treatment under the Internal Revenue Code, it doesn't have to meet the special requirements imposed on qualified plans. As a result, a nonqualified plan may discriminate between higher-paid and lower-paid employees. They can be set up to meet special compensation goals for specific employees.

Employers like such plans because they impose no administrative burden. There are no special rules to follow and no special government reporting requirements. Employees may also like such arrangements because it defers taxation on their compensation.

But there are risks. If the company has financial trouble, the promised compensation may never be paid. Creditors can claim the company's assets and wipe out the nonqualified plan participant's share.

A case in point is Edward Executive, a young, rising star with Tip Top Telecommunications, Inc. His salary and bonuses put him in the highest tax bracket, so he wanted a way to avoid taxes. Tip Top offered him the opportunity to defer up to 20% of his income until he retired at age 60 or older. After talking with his tax preparer, Ed told Tip Top "Yes!"

Things went well with this arrangement for the next three years. Then Tip Top hit a snag. They were sued for patent infringement — and lost. Bottom line, the company was put out of business overnight. Tip Top's creditors had first claim on all the company's assets. After they were through, Ed's deferred compensation was wiped out. So Ed has lost 20% of his big salary and he's out of a job, as well.

If your employer offers you a salary deferral plan, I think you'd be wise to think very long and very carefully about it. In this era of corporate takeovers and declining employer loyalty to employees, there are probably better plans for most people.

Some employers lower the risk, however, by funding these plans with cash value life insurance policies. (See Chapter 6.I. — Maybe So, Maybe Not — Cash Value Build-up Life Insurance Policies.)

In this kind of arrangement, known as a split dollar plan, the employer purchases a cash value life insurance policy with the employee's potential heirs as the designated beneficiaries. The employer pays the part of the premium that equals the annual increase in the cash value. The employee pays the balance of the premium.

This type of plan reduces the risk normally associated with Trust Me plans, but it is complicated. You should seek the advice of a qualified financial professional prior to entering into such an agreement.

Ready, Set, Retire!

6.E.
The Topless IRA

Tax-Deferred Annuities — Immediate, Fixed & Variable

Ratings

If invested in growth or equity type subaccounts:

Comfort	☺ ☺ ☺ ☺
Convenience	☺ ☺ ☺ ☺
Income & Appreciation	☺ ☺ ☺ ☺ ☺
Tax Savings	☺ ☺ ☺ ☺
Sex Appeal	☺ ☺ ☺ ☺

If invested in guaranteed or fixed income type subaccounts:

Comfort	☺ ☺ ☺ ☺ ☺
Convenience	☺ ☺ ☺ ☺
Income & Appreciation	☺ ☺
Tax Savings	☺ ☺ ☺ ☺
Sex Appeal	☺ ☺ ☺ ☺

If you like the tax deferral of an IRA or 401(k) Retirement Plan, you'll be even more excited about Tax-Deferred Annuities (TDAs). Unlike IRAs and

401(k) Plans which have limits on how much you can contribute every year, the TDA is topless. There's no limit to the amount of money you can stash away, tax-deferred, in a TDA. Further, an IRA requires you to begin taking money out and paying tax on it when you turn 70½. But you can leave the money in a TDA, tax-deferred, until you die.

A TDA is an account with an insurance company. You can purchase it in a lump sum through a single-premium contract, or in several payments through a flexible-premium contract. Your money will grow tax-deferred as long as it stays in the account.

TDAs have other advantages, as well. If you're already receiving Social Security benefits, TDAs may allow you to keep your current income below the level where Social Security benefits are taxed. Tax-free municipal bond interest, by contrast, is included in the calculations of Social Security income subject to income tax.

When you die, your TDA will normally be paid to your beneficiaries without the cost, delay and publicity of probate. Your beneficiaries can also choose the most tax-advantaged method to receive the TDA payout.

Like an IRA, once you withdraw money from a TDA, you'll pay tax on it.

Except for an Immediate Annuity, which is explained below, an early withdrawal from a TDA is penalized just like an IRA. You'll generally pay ordinary income tax plus a 10% penalty on any money you withdraw from a TDA prior to reaching 59½. So a TDA is clearly intended as a retirement investment, not a short-term parking place for money.

TDAs have a disadvantage when compared to capital gains. When you die, your beneficiaries *will not* have to pay income tax on any capital gains you have. Your beneficiaries *will* pay income tax on the earnings that have accumulated in your TDA account.

Let's distinguish between the various types of annuities.

Immediate Annuities

Like the name says, an Immediate Annuity begins to pay a monthly income immediately. You contract to deposit a certain amount of money with an insurance company. In turn, the insurance company agrees to pay you a monthly income for the rest of your life, or for a certain number of years, depending on the option that you select. The amount that the insurance company agrees to pay will depend on the amount of money you deposit, your sex, age, and the payment option that you select.

There are several things to consider before investing in an immediate annuity. The monthly payments are at least partly based on life expectancy. Someone in good health and with a family history of great longevity might find an immediate annuity to be an excellent investment. If you think that you may not live to a "normal" life expectancy, due to poor health, a family history of dying early, etc., an immediate annuity probably wouldn't be a good bet.

Immediate annuities also have a purchasing power risk. Since the monthly payments are fixed at the time of investment, they won't go up over time to offset the effects of inflation. The purchasing power of an immediate annuity's monthly payment will be cut in half in less than 16 years with 4.5% inflation.

It's also important to do a little shopping before investing your money. Rates change frequently. They also vary quite a bit from company to company. In addition, companies tend to be very competitive in the rates for some age brackets, but not for others.

As an example, I recently compared the monthly payment amounts for a 55 year old male among seven highly rated insurance companies. The difference was astounding. The highest monthly payment offered was 23.8% higher than the lowest rate offered! Like the song says, "You'd better shop around!"

Fixed Annuities

You can purchase a Fixed Annuity in a lump sum through a single-premium contract, or in several payments through a flexible-premium contract. Your money will grow tax-deferred as long as it stays in the account. Once you withdraw money, however, you'll pay tax on it.

So what's *fixed* about a Fixed Annuity? Fixed Annuities have an interest rate that is credited to your account on a periodic basis. The rate that's credited is *fixed* for a period of time, like 3 months, 1 year, 3 years, etc. Some Fixed Annuities are sold with a teaser rate (or bonus rate) that's higher than normal to start. The teaser rate then drops after a specified period of time.

Here again, you should shop for the best rates. Rate structures on fixed annuities can be a bit complicated. You should plan to spend some time comparing the alternatives.

There are also several features that might make a particular annuity better than others:

- Annuities with a bailout clause will allow you to cash in the annuity and get your money back without any penalty if the renewal rate paid on the annuity ever falls below a set level.

- An annuity with low surrender charges will give you greater flexibility. Most surrender charges range from 5% to 7% and may decline over 5 to 10 years.
- You'll also increase your flexibility if the annuity allows for annual 10% withdrawals without having to pay a penalty.

Variable Annuities

Like Fixed Annuities, you can purchase a Variable Annuity in a lump sum through a single-premium contract, or in several payments through a flexible-premium contract. Your money will grow tax-deferred as long as it stays in the account. Once you withdraw money, however, you'll pay tax on it.

Unlike Fixed Annuities, the rate of return you earn will fluctuate, and will depend on the investment performance of the various subaccounts within the annuity. Essentially, a variable annuity is like a family of mutual funds all wrapped up in an annuity package. The advantage is that you can get the growth potential of mutual funds combined with the tax-deferral of an annuity.

The rate of return isn't fixed on a Variable Annuity, so there is more risk. Since you have the potential for substantial, tax-deferred capital appreciation, however, a Variable Annuity may be ideally suited for a long-term retirement program. In this way, it is much like an IRA that's invested in mutual funds. As I mentioned at the beginning of this chapter, you get all of the advantages of an IRA. You also avoid some of the disadvantages.

Several insurance companies now offer variable annuities. Typically, the contract will allow you to select from among several investment alternatives. There will usually be at least a growth account, a growth and income account, and a fixed income account. Some contracts have twenty or more options, including foreign securities and precious metals.

There's also a "guaranteed death benefit" feature with many Variable Annuities. This feature says that if death occurs prior to a certain age, usually 75, the beneficiary will receive either the amount originally invested (the "floor" amount) or the current market value of the account — whichever is greater. Some contracts even allow for the "floor" amount to be adjusted upward every year or every few years. Still other contracts automatically raise the "floor" amount by a given percentage each year. The competition among insurance companies will undoubtedly produce other benefit enhancements in the future.

I think it would be wise for you to spend the time

to sit down with an insurance agent or stock broker who deals with annuities. They can explain the rates offered by various insurance companies and details about the special features of the annuities offered. Annuities are clearly more complicated than Certificates of Deposit from the friendly folks at First Last & Always Bank and Trust. However, the tax-deferral feature alone makes them worth the extra effort.

Finally, check the safety of any insurance company with whom you're contemplating investing money. After all, you want the insurance company to have a greater life expectancy than yours! The most feasible way for you to check on a company's safety is to look at how it's rated by the various independent rating firms. These firms generally do a pretty good job of evaluating the financial condition of insurance companies. But remember that they're not perfect, since no one has a perfect crystal ball.

The rating firms most widely used are A. M. Best Company, Standard & Poor's Corporation (S&P) and Moody's Investors Service. Duff & Phelps Credit Rating Company (D&P) and Weiss Research also rate insurance companies.

I think that an appropriate approach would be to select a company meeting this criterion:

The company must have very high ratings from two or three rating firms. Very high ratings would be as follows:

Best:	A++ or A+
S&P:	AAA, AA+ or AA
Moody's:	Aaa, Aa1, Aa2, or Aa3
D&P:	AAA or AA+
Weiss:	A+, A, A-, B+, B, or B-

There are over a hundred companies that meet this criterion.

How do you find out the ratings for a company? Simply ask the company or its agent to provide you with the ratings.

Ready, Set, Retire!

6.F.
The Good Got Better

Capital Gains

Ratings

Comfort	☺ ☺ ☺
Convenience	☺ ☺ ☺ ☺
Income & Appreciation	☺ ☺ ☺ ☺ ☺
Tax Savings	☺ ☺ ☺ ☺
Sex Appeal	☺ ☺ ☺ ☺

"Take home pay?" J.D. asked. "What's that?"

"Take home pay. You know, the money you have left in your paycheck after all the deductions."

"Paycheck?" J.D. asked. "What's that?"

"You know, the check you get each week for your pay."

"For my pay, I don't get a check each week!" J.D. said with a tone of contempt. "I get capital gains. And there aren't any deductions from my capital gains!"

This conversation supposedly took place between zillionaire John D. Rockefeller (J.D.) and an assistant.

True or not, it points out the simple fact that capital gains have generally had significant tax advantages over ordinary income.

The Congress has rewritten the tax laws affecting capital gains countless times over the years. Unless the folks from nearby St. Elizabeth's mental hospital go up to Capitol Hill and strap our elected *mis*representatives into straight jackets, they're likely to continue to keep changing them.

As I write this, long-term capital gains have two significant tax advantages over ordinary income. First, tax on the gain can be deferred. Second, the tax rate on capital gains is limited to 28%. This advantage is only a benefit to those in the 31%, 36% and 39.6% tax brackets.

Things like stocks, bonds and investment property are called capital assets in the tax laws. A long-term capital gain is when a capital asset that has been held for more than one year goes up in value, i.e. when it appreciates. When that happens, the tax laws grant the asset's owner two tax breaks. First, you don't pay any tax on that increase (appreciation) in value until you sell the asset. So you get to defer paying any tax on the appreciation until you have realized it through an actual sale. (This is probably where the distinction between real gains and paper gains comes from. If you haven't actually sold the asset at a gain, it's still a paper gain, not a real one.)

When you sell the appreciated asset, you'll pay capital gains tax. Since the tax on capital gains is limited to 28%, a taxpayer in the 31%, 36% or 39.6% bracket will have a tax advantage to invest in assets that generate capital gains rather than income. If you're a higher brackets taxpayer, for example, it will be to your advantage to have your portfolio invested in growth stocks and other appreciating assets rather than in assets that produce large dividends and interest income.

A portfolio of bonds that produces a return of 9% per year in the form of interest income and 0% in capital appreciation will only give a 36% bracket taxpayer a 5.76% return after taxes ([1.00 - .36] times 9% = 5.76%). On the other hand, a stock that rises 9% in value over a year's time and pays no dividends will produce an after-tax return of 6.48% ([1.00 - .28] times 9% = 6.48%). So here you have two assets that produce the *same gain before taxes*. But the asset that produces a long-term capital gain will give the 36% bracket taxpayer *12.5% more money after taxes* ([6.48%-5.76%]/5.76% = 12.5%).

Even better, if that appreciated stock isn't sold, *all of the gain is deferred until the time when it is sold.* This deferral, as we've already discussed, is a huge benefit, since it allows the gains to compound faster over time.

"Whoa, pardner!" Our conscientious buddy, Mr. Discouraging Word, just looked over my shoulder and reminded me that assets that produce capital *gains* can also produce capital *losses*.

"True enough," I say. "Capital assets sometimes lose value. When they do, you can deduct those losses from the gains on other assets."

"But you may not have any gains on other assets," Discouraging says, thumping his chest.

"Well, then, you can offset your capital losses against your ordinary income from your job," I say.

"Hold on a minute there," Discouraging counters. "You can only offset up to $3,000 of ordinary income each year. If you have more than that, you'll have to carry the extra losses over to subsequent years."

"So you'd better be prudent in selecting capital assets for appreciation," I suggest.

"You bet!" Mr. Discouraging Word concludes.

Then Mr. Happy Trails stops in to offer his observations. "Mutual funds offer a prudent way to take advantage of capital gains tax rates," he says.

"True, they're prudent, alright," I say. "They offer professional management, broad diversification, easy reinvestment of dividend income, and a very flexible and convenient method of investing for long-term goals."

"Hrrummpf!" Mr. Discouraging Word scoffs. "They may be prudent, but mutual funds got hit by those nasty Congressional Revenue Hunters a while back."

"How's that?" Happy asks.

"Well, it used to be," Discouraging begins, "that mutual funds didn't have to distribute the capital gains they'd earned on the stocks they'd sold. They could just keep rolling those gains over into other stocks, deferring the gains forever."

"Then what happened?" Happy asks.

"A few years ago, the Congressional Revenue Hunters took aim at mutual funds and forced them to distribute the capital gains every year."

"Technically," I say, "they're required to either distribute to their shareholders substantially all of the capital gains they've earned during the year or to pay a tax on those gains. Since it's in the best interests of the shareholders to distribute the gains, that's what the funds generally do."

"So you can't get the advantage of tax deferral on the capital gains?" Happy asks.

"That's right," Discouraging says.

"You can't if you just own mutual funds in an ordinary way," I say. "But if you own them inside an IRA, a 401(k) Plan, or even in a Tax-Deferred Annuity, you *do* get tax deferral."

"I guess there's more than one way to skin a cat."
Happy smiles. (My apologies to Garfield, Morris,
Sylvester and all their feline kin.)

6.G.
Good Enough To Die For

Capital Gains, When Held Until Death

Ratings

Comfort	☺ ☺ ☺
Convenience	☺ ☺ ☺ ☺ ☺
Income & Appreciation	☺ ☺ ☺ ☺ ☺
Tax Savings	☺ ☺ ☺ ☺ ☺
Sex Appeal	☺ ☺ ☺ ☺ ☺

The amount of a capital gain is the difference between its "cost basis" and its "sale proceeds." Suppose you buy a share of Thrill-A-Minit Whoopee Cushions, Inc. stock for $50 and pay a commission of $1 when you buy the share. A couple of years later you decide to sell the share of stock for $75 and you pay a $1.50 commission to sell it. Here are the details:

Cost Basis Calculation:
Purchase Price	$50.00
Plus:	
Expenses of acquisition	1.00
Cost Basis	$51.00

Sale Proceeds Calculation:

Sale Price	$75.00
Less:	
Expenses of disposal	1.50
Sale Proceeds	$73.50
Capital Gain	$22.50

Now let's change the facts a little bit. Suppose your dear old Aunt Minnie was the person who'd bought this Thrill-A-Minit Whoopee Cushion stock. She is a jolly old lady, after all. Then, after a thrilling ride that lasted an hour beyond the manufacturer's recommended whoopee session, old Aunt Minnie's heart gave out and she died. The Thrill-A-Minit stock would go to Aunt Minnie's heirs — you — with a new, stepped-up cost basis. Generally, your cost basis in the inherited stock would be its "fair market value" at the time of Aunt Minnie's death.

Isn't the IRS generous? Aunt Minnie didn't have to pay any taxes on the gain in her Thrill-A-Minit Whoopee Cushion stock. All she had to do to get this generosity was to die!

But watch out. The Congressional Revenue Hunters may try to focus their sights on this one. These intrepid stalkers have been looking fondly lately at opportunities to tax the dead. Yes, it was just a matter of time. The dead don't vote, they figure, at least not outside of Chicago. But, hey, that's another story.

Now let's change the facts once again. Suppose that Aunt Minnie gave the stock to you long before she died. In that case, there may not be a change in the cost basis. If you sell the stock at a gain, you use Aunt Minnie's cost basis. If you sell it at a loss, the cost basis is either Aunt Minnie's basis or the fair market value at the time of the gift, whichever is *lower*.

For example, assume these values:

Aunt Minnie's Cost Basis	$51
Fair Market Value at time of Aunt Minnie's gift	$60
Stock price when you sell it, adjusted for sales expenses	$81

Since you sold the stock at a gain ($81), you use Aunt Minnie's basis ($51) and pay tax on the difference ($81 - $51 = $30).

Now what happens if you sell it at $45 instead of $81? In this case, since you're selling at a loss, you use for the cost basis either Aunt Minnie's basis ($51) or the fair market value at the time of the gift ($60), again whichever is lower. Since Aunt Minnie's basis ($51) is lower, that's the basis you use. So your loss for tax purposes is Aunt Minnie's basis less the price you sell the stock for ($51 -$45 = $6).

Do you see what a rotten trick this is? If there's a gain, it's the biggest gain possible so the IRS collects the most tax. If there's a loss, it's the smallest loss possible, so the IRS loses the least tax from the loss deduction. This is the IRS equivalent of heads the IRS wins, tails the taxpayer loses.

Fortunately, this scenario can frequently be avoided. If an elderly person like Aunt Minnie owns a capital asset with a large capital gain, she probably shouldn't give it away to an heir. Unless the potential heir really needs the proceeds from selling the asset now, the heir will likely end up with far more money if he or she simply waits to receive the asset through Aunt Minnie's estate.

Now granted, this arrangement requires a bit of trust on Aunt Minnie's part and a bit of restraint on the part of her heirs. After all, it creates a sort of "vested interest" in her demise for those who will inherit her capital assets!

But seriously, I've seen a lot of families foul this up. In an effort to avoid the complications of probate, a lot of parents with adult children will simply add their children's names as joint tenants to the titles of certain capital assets — like the parent's house. True, the house will then pass to the children without probate. But the change in title is a gift. And the house has probably appreciated in value substantially since the parents bought it. The title change means the children will now have to pay capital gains tax on their proportionate share of the appreciation. If the children receive the house through the estate, the gain will go untaxed due to the step-up in cost basis at the parent's time of death. A little forethought in estate planning can avoid a mistake like this.

My advice here is simple and blunt. Before you transfer title to an appreciated asset, consult a tax professional. The few nickels you spend on a consultation could save you and your heirs a lot of dollars.

6.H.
Better Than Underwear
On Christmas Morning

Series EE U. S. Government Bonds

Ratings

Comfort	☺ ☺ ☺ ☺ ☺
Convenience	☺ ☺ ☺ ☺
Income & Appreciation	☺
Tax Savings	☺ ☺ ☺ ☺
Sex Appeal	☺

Your dear old Aunt Minnie probably gave you some Series EE bonds for Christmas when you were a little kid. Never mind that what you really wanted was a snazzy, red two-wheeler with streamers coming out of the handlebars and reflectors in the spokes that made a whistling sound when you rode it. It could have been worse. She could have given you underwear!

When she gave you Series EE bonds, Aunt Minnie was giving you an investment that offers tax-deferral of income for those seeking investments that are small in size and safe in terms of loss of principal or interest.

These bonds come in the following denominations:

Cost Price	Face Amount
25.00	50.00
37.50	75.00
50.00	100.00
100.00	200.00
250.00	500.00
500.00	1,000.00
2,500.00	5,000.00
5,000.00	10,000.00

Purchases are limited, however, to $30,000 (face amount) per person in any one calendar year. There is no cumulative limit on the amount an individual can purchase.

These bonds are guaranteed against loss of principal and interest by the federal government. They're safe, too, if they're lost in a fire or flood, or through theft or vandalism. Even if Aunt Minnie hears you complaining about those "boring bonds again" (shame on you!) and tears them up, the government will replace them free of charge and with no loss of principal or interest.

Series EE bonds are relatively liquid. They can be redeemed after 6 months. If cashed in prior to 5 years, however, the rate of interest earned is sharply reduced.

So these bonds are best suited for investments of 5 years or more. In fact, if you'd been patient enough, you could have cashed in those "boring bonds" for a snazzy, red *four*-wheeler when you got your driver's license — and your parents' permission.

Like all U.S. Government bonds, the interest on Series EE bonds is not taxable by your state of residence.

The best part about Series EE bonds, however, is that YOU decide when to pay the tax on the interest they earn. You can pay it currently, in the year you earn it, if you want. If you're a youngster without much other income, that might be a good idea, since you can have up to $600 of income each year tax free!

You may choose, instead, to defer the tax on the interest until you cash in the bond. This would be a good idea if you want the money to keep growing inside the bond and avoid current taxes.

You can even go further and reinvest the proceeds from cashing in Series EE bonds into Series *HH* bonds. The reinvested interest isn't taxed until the Series *HH* bonds mature. You could, for example, defer paying income tax on your Series EE bond interest until you retire, then cash them in and reinvest the money into Series HH bonds. You could then use the Series HH bond interest payments to live on and further defer payment of taxes on the Series EE interest for up to 20 years. Wouldn't Aunt Minnie be proud of you if you did that?!

Like all good things, however, there's a catch with Series EE bonds. The problem is that the interest rate is only 85% of the average return during the period of time covered by the bond on marketable Treasury securities with five years remaining to their maturity, or 4%, whichever is higher. This is a complicated way of saying that you'll earn interest at either 4% or at 85% of whatever the average rate is on five year Treasury securities — whichever is higher. Since five year Treasuries offer a comparatively low rate of return, and the Series EE rate is limited to 85% of that low rate (subject to the 4% floor), I can't see anyone getting very excited about these bonds.

Series EE U. S. Government Bonds —
When Used To Pay College Tuition & Fees

Ratings

Comfort	☺ ☺ ☺ ☺ ☺
Convenience	☺ ☺ ☺ ☺
Income & Appreciation	☺
Tax Savings	☺ ☺ ☺ ☺ ☺
Sex Appeal	☺

Why are we even talking about using Series EE bonds for college education funding when this is a book about retirement planning? It's simple, really. If you have kids who will be going to college some day, and you expect to pay part or all of the tab, you could wind up blowing the better part of your retirement nest egg on college expenses. For proof, just ask friends or relatives who are currently living with the sticker shock of college tuition costs.

My best advice is to separate your retirement funds from your college education funds. The temptation to mingle them will be greatest during your children's college years. The price for that mingling might just turn out to be 25 years of retirement in financial misery while your children are enjoying world-wide travel junkets won through their expensive educations! Or, worse, you could become financially dependent upon children who are highly educated yet underemployed, and thus not able to support you.

So, for those who are still facing the financial challenge of funding college educations, I've included this section on using Series EE bonds to generate tax-free tuition money.

- o - o - o -

For some taxpayers, the interest on EE Bonds may be tax-free if the bonds are used for college tuition and fees. There are several restrictions and conditions, however:

- The bond must have been issued after 1989.
- The bond purchaser must be at least 24 years old when he or she purchases it.
- The bond must be held in an adult's name and be redeemed by that adult.
- The bond proceeds must be used for tuition and fees for either the bond owner, the bond owner's spouse, or dependent. Bond proceeds may not be used for other educational expenses, like room, board, books, midnight pizza deliveries, "essential" sports equipment, the latest in what masquerades for music, or other living expenses.
- To be tax-free, the bonds redeemed plus interest

may not be greater than the actual covered tuition and fees in the year of the bond redemption.

- The tax-free status of the bonds is subject to an income test on the bond owner in the year the bond is redeemed and the tuition and fees are paid. Please refer to the table below:

Income Range		Tax Status of Interest
Single or Joint Filer	Head of Household	
Up to $68,250	Up to $45,500	Totally Tax-Free
$68,250-98,250	$45,500-60,500	Partially Tax-Free
Over $98,250	Over $60,500	Totally Taxable

As long as the government can afford it and the politicians don't discover it as another source of revenue, these amounts are subject to an annual adjustment for inflation.

The tax-free appeal of Series EE bonds when used for college expenses should be weighed against other considerations:

- How likely is it that Congress will leave the tax-free income ranges alone?
- How likely are you to be in the required tax-free or partially tax-free income range when you need to redeem the bonds to pay for college expenses?

- After considering the various risks involved, is the rate you can earn on the bonds comparable to the rate on other alternatives?
- How likely is it that you'll actually use the bonds to pay for college expenses? Remember, if you don't use them for college tuition and fees, they're not tax-free.

After examining all of these factors, many people will justifiably conclude that Series EE bonds are not a very good investment. The potential negatives may considerably outweigh the positives.

(Please also read the discussion on how Series EE bond interest is calculated in the previous section, "Series EE U. S. Government Bonds.")

6.I.
Maybe So, Maybe Not

Cash Value Build-up
Life Insurance Policies

Ratings

Comfort	☺ ☺ ☺ ☺ ☺
Convenience	☺ ☺ ☺
Income & Appreciation	☺ ☺
Tax Savings	☺ ☺ ☺
Sex Appeal	☺

It used to be that nearly everyone bought what's known as Whole Life Insurance. In such a policy, you pay a premium for the rest of your life. When you die, the insurance company pays your heirs the stated amount of the policy.

Policies like this weren't terribly popular with the person to be insured, however, and still aren't for many people. I remember the story of a gentleman who had an amusing response to an approach by a young life insurance agent. "Sonny," he said, "I don't want any life insurance."

"Why's that?" the insurance agent asked.

"Because when I die, I want *everybody* to be unhappy."

To counteract this problem, insurance agents were trained to point out the savings feature of the policy. "A piece of each premium goes toward your *cash value*," the agent would explain.

Over time, the cash value builds. "And you can borrow that cash if you need it," the agent would say.

What wasn't stated, however, is that the cash value won't be growing very much while in the policy. The insurance company may not even disclose how much it will be crediting to the cash value over time.

Many people also wrongly assumed that the policy would pay both the stated death benefit *and* the accumulated cash value. The truth is that it will never pay more than the face amount of the policy. If the policyholder borrows from the policy and the loan is still outstanding, the loan amount is subtracted from the face amount before it is paid.

Nowadays, insurance agents are much less likely to encourage you to purchase a whole life policy. Still, a whole life policy does have some attractive features for some types of people.

- It provides a disciplined way to save money for those who need an enforced savings plan.

- The cash value in the policy will grow tax-deferred.

- The cash value can be borrowed from the policy. Since it is a loan, it is a tax-free source of cash.

- The policy is permanent insurance — it will not run out when you get older, as term insurance does.

Fortunately, other forms of life insurance offer these same advantages without some of the disadvantages. Universal life insurance policies, for example, can be structured to offer all of these benefits. And the rate of return credited on the policy's cash value is disclosed.

With universal life you also have the flexibility of changing the amount of your premium. You can add more money to the policy, for example, to increase the cash value. Or you can skip some premiums. Be careful with this feature, however, since too many missed premiums will cause the policy to lapse.

As you can see, the idea of a life insurance policy building a tax-deferred cash value is a good one. But it is important to choose the best type of policy in which to build that cash value. Fortunately, the insurance industry has responded with a large array of policies that will meet both pure insurance needs and cash savings needs.

Most life insurance agents will be happy to discuss the *insurance* and *savings* features of a variety of policies. Make sure you understand both elements of any policy you buy.

See a discussion of other forms of cash value life insurance in Chapters 6.C. — Cut the Red Tape, 6.D. — "Trust Me" Plans, and 6.J. — The Jackpot.

6.J.
The Jackpot

Variable Universal Life Insurance Policies

Ratings

If invested in growth or equity type subaccounts:

Comfort	☺ ☺ ☺ ☺
Convenience	☺ ☺
Income & Appreciation	☺ ☺ ☺ ☺ ☺
Tax Savings	☺ ☺ ☺ ☺ ☺
Sex Appeal	☺ ☺ ☺ ☺ ☺

If invested in guaranteed or fixed income type subaccounts:

Comfort	☺ ☺ ☺ ☺ ☺
Convenience	☺ ☺
Income & Appreciation	☺ ☺
Tax Savings	☺ ☺ ☺ ☺ ☺
Sex Appeal	☺ ☺ ☺ ☺ ☺

A Variable Universal Life Insurance Policy is, in essence, a family of mutual funds wrapped inside a life insurance policy package. The advantage is that you can get the growth potential of mutual funds combined with the tax-deferred growth and tax-free income benefits of an insurance policy.

Since the rate of return isn't fixed on a Variable Universal Life Insurance Policy, there is more risk than with a regular Universal Life policy. With that risk, however, you have the potential for substantial, tax-deferred (or even tax-free) capital appreciation. So a Variable policy may be ideally suited for a long-term retirement program. You get all of the advantages of an IRA that's invested in mutual funds. You also avoid some of the disadvantages, like paying tax when you withdraw money.

Money paid into a Variable Universal Life policy will grow tax-deferred. Money can be borrowed out at any time, although there are some restrictions on the amount. Since the borrowed money is a loan, it's considered tax-free.

You may use money in the policy to pay for a child's college expenses, for example. Then, at retirement, you can dip into the policy again to provide retirement income. In the meantime, the policy continues to provide some life insurance coverage.

Several insurance companies now offer Variable Universal Life policies. The policy will normally allow you to select from among several investment alternatives. There will usually be at least a growth account, a growth and income account, and a fixed income account. Some contracts have twenty or more options, including foreign securities and precious metals.

In selecting the investment accounts to use for such a policy, I'd strongly suggest that you follow the *Five Steps For Comfortable Investing* listed in Chapter 2 on Understanding Risk.

As I discussed in Chapter 6.C. — Cut the Red Tape, beware of the Fantastic Forecast that an insurance agent may show you. Ask the agent to show you illustrations using 7-10% rate of return assumptions. Those percentages should be realistic over the long term for a diversified portfolio of subaccounts.

You should also remember the importance of the policy's net interest charge. As I showed in Chapter 6.C. — Cut the Red Tape, a very small net interest charge on borrowing from the policy can make a very big difference in the total amount that can be borrowed.

Remember, too, that these policies work best as investment vehicles for people under age 55. And you should only buy a policy from a financially strong insurance company. See Chapter 6.C. — Cut the Red Tape for a fuller discussion of insurance policy cautions.

If you're willing to go through the somewhat lengthy process of shopping for a good Variable Universal Life policy, you'll probably be rewarded with what I regard as the Jackpot of investments. You get the right to unlimited contributions, tax-deferred growth, tax-free income, growth similar to common stock mutual funds, great flexibility, and some life insurance coverage, too. What's more, there's no government red tape to worry about and no tax reporting requirements.

6.K.
Tax-Free In Four Flavors

6.K.1.
Municipal Bonds - Same State as Residence

Ratings

Comfort	☺ ☺ ☺ ☺
Convenience	☺ ☺ ☺ ☺
Income & Appreciation	☺ ☺
Tax Savings	☺ ☺ ☺ ☺ ☺
Sex Appeal	☺ ☺

Imagine you've had a hard day and you've just started the entrée of a delicious, home cooked, birthday dinner. It's a pleasure to relax over a leisurely meal with your spouse.

"I sure appreciate the extra touches, honey," you say. "The candlelight really sets the mood." Your romantic juices are starting to flow.

"I just wanted to do something nice for your birthday," your spouse says. "Would you like a massage after we eat?" Would you! ☺!

Then, from the kitchen you hear "Rrrrrring! Rrrrrring!" You both pause. Drat!

"I'll get it," you volunteer, without really meaning it. "Hello. Yes, this is Pat Pantstingle."

"How would you like some tax-free income?" the caller asks.

"I'm in the middle of dinner," you mumble.

"Well I have a new bond from your state that'll pay you 6.5%, tax-free! The bonds are rated double-A and come in $5,000 denominations. How many would you be interested in, $25,000?"

"Who is this?" you ask.

"Oh, I'm sorry," the voice says brightly. "This is Malcolm Motormouth with Findem, Grabem & Sellem Securities. These tax-free bonds are selling fast. How many can I save for you?"

"Look, I don't want any of your #&$*!$#@%! tax-free bonds. And don't call me again!"

Click!

I think it's unfortunate that so many people are introduced to tax-free bonds in just this way. Well, maybe not exactly *this* way, but you know what I mean. Anyway, tax-free bonds are one of the favorite financial products of rookie brokers (and some veteran brokers, too).

They sound safe. They're bonds, after all, not those risky stocks. They're probably issued and backed by your state of residence, so they're local and, therefore, more familiar than an investment from someplace far away. They pay income, and that certainly sounds better than having to depend on capital appreciation that might never happen. Best of all, the income these bonds pay is totally tax-free.

Now don't misunderstand me. I think tax-free municipal bonds are a great investment for some people. If you have lots of money — like Ross Perot, for instance — and your primary concerns are preservation of your principal and avoiding income taxes, then municipal bonds are wonderful. A well-diversified portfolio of high quality municipal bonds should allow anyone to sleep well at night, even Ross Perot — after he's checked under his bed for spies or whatever. And you certainly won't have to worry about paying any income taxes on the bonds since bonds from your state of residence are totally tax-free.

What I'm concerned about is whether municipal bonds are an appropriate investment for someone trying to build a retirement nest egg. Historically, the rate of return on municipal bonds hasn't been sufficient to offset the ravages of inflation. As a result, the purchasing power of money invested in municipal bonds has remained relatively stagnant, rather than growing.

I'm also not sure that municipal bonds are an appropriate place to preserve the purchasing power of an established retirement nest egg. Unless you're very old, in very poor health, or have a lot of money, the stagnant purchasing power value of a municipal bond portfolio may cause your retirement fund to shrink and disappear long before you retire to your heavenly rocking chair.

It could get even worse. You may have joined the great yield chase that occurs when interest rates decline. In your search for a better rate of return, you may have put a sizable amount of your funds into long-term municipal bonds (20 and 30 year maturity). By doing that, you probably added a percentage point or two to your rate of return. But you did it at the risk of losing 10% to 35% (or more) of the value of your portfolio.

Let me explain. Consider what would happen if interest rates available in the marketplace increase again. A meager one percentage point increase in interest rates, for example, will cause the value of a typical 20-year bond to drop in value by 10% to 12%. A 30-year bond will drop even more. To most of the people with whom I've worked over the years, a 10-12% drop is catastrophic. How would *you* feel?

To avoid this risk, I think it is prudent to avoid long-term bonds when interest rates are low. At such times, long-term bond interest rates may *appear* much more attractive. But I just don't often see them high enough to compensate for the increased risk.

There are generally two types of municipal bonds. General Obligation Bonds are issued by states, cities, and counties. They're backed by the full taxing ability of the issuer. Revenue Bonds, in contrast, are backed only by the income produced by projects like hospitals, universities, airports, housing development mortgages, or toll roads and bridges.

An issuing state, city or county can merely raise taxes, if necessary, to meet its obligations on a general obligation bond. These bonds carry a relatively small credit risk. On the other hand, since revenue bonds are more likely to default on interest and principal payments, they're a poorer credit risk. If a hospital is unprofitable, for example, it may be difficult for it to raise prices or cut expenses enough to provide the income to pay off the revenue bond that built it.

Municipal bonds have usually been thought of as safe investments. Over the past decade, however, the federal government has mandated many expensive programs at the state and local level. At the same time, the federal government has often failed to provide any money to pay for these programs. Perhaps as a result, there have been an increasing number of municipal bond defaults.

Many elderly Social Security recipients view tax-free municipal bonds as their favorite investments. Those sharp-eyed Congressional Revenue Hunters caught sight of this fact, however, and fired a ricochet shot right in the gut of higher income Social Security recipients. The interest on tax-free municipal bonds isn't taxed directly, of course. Those crafty Congressional Revenue Hunters are too clever for that. Instead, they've merely included tax-free interest in the income that's counted to determine how much of your Social Security income will be taxed. (As I noted in the section on Tax-Deferred Annuities, if you're already receiving Social Security benefits, TDAs may allow you to keep your current income below the level where Social Security benefits are taxed.)

You should also be aware of "bond calls." If a bond has a "call" feature, the issuer will have the right to call, or buy back, the bond at a specific price at a specified time prior to the maturity date. If a company or municipality issues bonds at a time when interest rates are high, for example, it may want the right to buy them back if interest rates fall in the future. This will allow the issuer to replace the old, expensive bonds with new, less expensive, lower interest rate bonds. The issuer will thereby save some money.

From the investor point of view, however, this isn't a very good deal. Imagine, for example, that you bought a municipal bond with an interest rate of 10%. Then, over the next few years, the interest rates on new municipal bonds dropped to 6%. You'd feel pretty lucky to have your 10% bond, wouldn't you? If your bonds have a call feature, however, they can be called away from you. If new bonds can be sold to the public at a 6% interest rate, I virtually can assure you that your 10% bonds will be called if they are callable. The issuer would be crazy not to. So wham, just when you thought you'd locked up a great interest rate for a long, long time, the bond issuer buys them back from you and stops your high-interest gravy train right in its tracks.

Let's look at a little different situation. Suppose you bought $10,000 worth of bonds when interest rates were 6%. At the time, your $600 in annual interest payments looked pretty good. Over the next few years, however, interest rates on new municipal bonds rose to 10%. The issuer certainly wouldn't call your low-interest bonds. The issuer got the money far more cheaply than it could with new bonds now. You'd like to get out of your 6% bonds and buy some of these newer 10% bonds. I have some bad news. Your 6% bonds have dropped about 40% in value, from about $10,000 to $6,000. That's because anyone buying bonds now wants to get 10% interest. Since your 6% bonds only pay $600 per year, that $600 is 10% of only $6,000. So that's all that someone would be willing to pay you.

Talk about a rotten deal! A callable bond is stacked against you. If interest rates go down, they'll call your high-interest rate bond away from you. If interest rates go up, you'll be stuck with a low-interest bond that's dropped in value. This is a real heads they win, tails you lose situation.

Do you want a way to beat this rigged game? Securities issued by the U.S. Treasury may be the answer. Unlike municipal bonds, *Treasuries can't ever be called away from you.* Consider this question: When is a 10 year maturity bond paying a 15% *taxable* interest rate better than a 10 year maturity bond paying a 14% *tax-free* interest rate? The answer may be: When the 15% bond lasts for 10 years and the 14% bond gets called away after only 2 years.

Now, after I've said all of these not-so-flattering things about municipal bonds, let me say a few kind words. I think short-term and intermediate-term municipal bonds (i.e. maturities of 5-10 years or so) are an excellent alternative to other, taxable short-term and intermediate-term investments, like certificates of deposit. To make my point, please look at the following table, and find your income tax bracket.

Tax-Free In Four Flavors

Marital Status	Taxable Income Range			Tax Rate
Single:	0	to	22,100	15.0%
Married:	0	to	36,900	15.0%
Single:	22,101	to	53,500	28.0%
Married:	36,901	to	89,150	28.0%
Single:	53,501	to	115,000	31.0%
Married:	89,151	to	140,000	31.0%
Single:	115,001	to	250,000	36.0%
Married:	140,001	to	250,000	36.0%
Single:	250,001	and	Over	39.6%
Married:	250,001	and	Over	39.6%

Now look at the next table to see what a taxable investment would have to give you in interest to equal the indicated tax-free interest rates.

Tax	In your tax bracket, a tax-free interest yield of...					
	4.0%	5.0%	6.0%	7.0%	8.0%	9.0%
Bracket	equals the taxable investment yield of...					
15.0%	4.7%	5.9%	7.1%	8.2%	9.4%	10.6%
28.0%	5.6%	6.9%	8.3%	9.7%	11.1%	12.5%
31.0%	5.8%	7.2%	8.7%	10.1%	11.6%	13.0%
36.0%	6.3%	7.8%	9.4%	10.9%	12.5%	14.1%
39.6%	6.6%	8.3%	9.9%	11.6%	13.2%	14.9%

Simply stated, if you're in the 28% tax bracket, you would need a 6.9% interest rate on a certificate of deposit (CD) from First Last & Always Bank and Trust to equal a 5.00% rate on a tax-free municipal bond. For taxpayers in the 28% or higher brackets, the after-tax return from municipal bond interest rates will usually be higher than what's available from taxable investment interest rates.

See for yourself. Call those friendly folks down at First Last & Always Bank and Trust and get their 5-year CD rates. Then call a broker who competes with that obnoxious Malcolm Motormouth from Findem, Grabem & Sellem Securities, and ask for rates on a AAA-rated, 5-year municipal bond. I'm sure the answer won't make you as happy as a massage after dinner. But I think you'll find that you can make more money from the municipal bonds than you can from the CDs.

Tax-Free In Four Flavors

Many investors are reluctant to buy bonds that are priced at a premium to their face value, e.g. a price of 102 for a bond with a face value of 100. Instead, they usually prefer to buy bonds that are priced at a discount to their face value, e.g. a price of 98 for a face value of 100. This preference results from a misunderstanding of what's being bought.

What you're buying is the *after-tax yield to maturity*. Let's use an example. Suppose your broker shows you two possible bonds.

Terms of the Bonds	Bond A	Bond B
Maturity Term	1 year	1 year
Coupon Interest Rate	5%	9%
Interest in Dollars	$ 5	$ 9
Price	$ 98	$102

If you buy both bonds, what will you get over the life of each one?

	Bond A	Bond B
Purchase Cost	$(98.00)	$(102.00)
Interest Received	$ 5.00	$ 9.00
Face Value at Maturity	$ 100.00	$ 100.00
Net Gain	$ 7.00	$ 7.00

It looks the same, doesn't it? But the tax laws say its not! On Bond A, you had a taxable gain. Bond B gave you a taxable loss. Let's see how it looks *after* taxes.

	Bond A	Bond B
Purchase Cost	$(98.00)	$(102.00)
Interest Received	$ 5.00	$ 9.00
Purchase Price Returned at Maturity	$ 98.00	$ 100.00
Gain Paid at Maturity	$ 2.00	$ 0.00
Savings on Loss of Purchase Price (28% Tax Bracket)	$ 0.00	$ .56
Tax Cost of Gain on Purchase Price (28% Tax Bracket)	$(.56)	$ 0.00
Net Gain After Tax	$ 6.44	$ 7.56

So Bond A, the one bought at a discount, only returned $6.44 after tax, i.e. an after-tax yield of 6.44%. Bond B, the one bought at a premium, returned $7.56, i.e. an after-tax yield of 7.56%.

- o - o - o -

Finally, for you mathematically inclined types, here are the formulas you can use for calculating the taxable equivalent yield and tax-free equivalent yield of an investment.

Tax-Free In Four Flavors

Where: T   = Federal Income Tax Rate
           Yield   = Interest Rate

$$\text{Taxable Investment Yield Equivalent to Tax-Free Investment} = \frac{\text{Tax-Free Investment Interest Rate}}{(1 - T)}$$

$$\text{Tax-Free Investment Yield Equivalent to Taxable Investment} = \text{Taxable Interest Rate} \times (1 - T)$$

Now, go forth and multiply!

Ready, Set, Retire!

6.K.2.
Municipal Bonds — NOT Same State As Residence

Ratings

Comfort	☺ ☺ ☺ ☺
Convenience	☺ ☺ ☺ ☺
Income & Appreciation	☺ ☺
Tax Savings	☺ ☺ ☺ ☺
Sex Appeal	☺ ☺

As I've said, bonds from your own state pay you interest that is totally tax-free, i.e. no federal income tax and no state or local income tax either. So why would someone buy municipal bonds from a state where they don't live? One reason is that there are still a few states where there's no state income tax. In those states, there wouldn't be any state tax on an out-of-state bond anyway.

It could also be that the interest rate on an out-of-state bond is high enough to give you a better deal than your own state's bonds, even after you deduct your state income tax from the out-of-state bond. Your broker will usually be happy to do the calculations for you to see which kind of bond gives you the greatest after-tax rate of return.

Another reason to buy an out-of-state bond is that you may be nervous about the safety of the bonds from your state. Each state has its unique financial strengths and weaknesses. Some have to get voter approval for bond issues; some don't. Some have to get voter approval for tax levies; others don't. If you're from a state that's weak financially, it may be wise for you to buy another state's bonds, even if the after-tax yield is lower. I think it's prudent to accept a somewhat lower yield than to risk losing all of your principal.

There's also the issue of diversification. You may feel that putting all of your municipal bond money in one state is risky. Spreading your investments among several states may be a wise alternative.

6.K.3.
Municipal Bond Unit Investment Trusts — Insured and Non-insured; Same State As Residence Or National

---

Ratings

Comfort	☺ ☺ ☺ ☺ ☺
Convenience	☺ ☺ ☺ ☺ ☺
Income & Appreciation	☺ ☺
Tax Savings	☺ ☺ ☺ ☺
Sex Appeal	☺ ☺ ☺

Do you want to buy some bonds but don't have much money to invest? Well, those clever folks on Wall Street have just the answer for you. It's called the Unit Investment Trust (UIT). It's really nothing more than a group of bonds, all wrapped up in a single package, and sold in units.

A UIT has some advantages over buying individual bonds. If you're a person with a very limited amount to invest, the UIT will give you the diversification of several bonds for a small investment. Further, bonds are selected by bond professionals to meet specified interest rate, risk and maturity criteria. You can buy UITs that are made up solely of bonds from your home state, or from a cross-section of states. You can buy UITs that are either insured or uninsured as to payment of interest and principal. Finally, UITs come in a variety of maturities, from 3 to 30 years.

There is a downside, however. A UIT is a fixed portfolio of bonds. Once they're packaged as a UIT, they generally aren't managed by anyone. Interest payments are collected and distributed to the unit holders. When bonds in the UIT mature, the principal is distributed to the investors. In the meantime, however, there's very little, if any, attempt to monitor the bonds in the UIT. If there is a deterioration in the credit quality of a particular bond's issuer, there's nobody managing the UIT to do anything about it. The bond simply stays in the UIT.

I personally don't think this is a risk that's any greater than the way most investors manage a portfolio of individual bonds. Most investors, from my experience, buy bonds and hold them until they mature. Along the way, they pay very little attention to the bonds. As a result, the individual investors who hold bonds that end up defaulting are usually very surprised. They had no idea that there were potential problems with their bonds.

Another downside with UITs versus individual bonds, however, is that UITs frequently carry a somewhat higher transaction charge. If you can afford to invest $100,000 or so in municipal bonds, you can often get both adequate diversification and lower overall transaction costs from a portfolio of individual bonds. If you have smaller amounts to invest, however, a UIT's possibly higher transaction cost is probably justified by the added diversification you'll receive.

6.K.4.
Municipal Bond Mutual Funds — Same State As Residence Or National

Ratings

	Same State	National
Comfort	☺☺☺☺☺	☺☺☺☺☺
Convenience	☺☺☺☺☺	☺☺☺☺☺
Income & Appreciation	☺☺	☺☺
Tax Savings	☺☺☺☺☺	☺☺☺☺
Sex Appeal	☺☺☺	☺☺☺

	Short-Term	Long-term
Comfort	☺☺☺☺☺	☺☺☺
Convenience	☺☺☺☺☺	☺☺☺☺☺
Income & Appreciation	☺☺	☺☺☺
Tax Savings	☺☺☺☺	☺☺☺☺
Sex Appeal	☺☺	☺☺☺

Do you want your municipal bond portfolio managed by a bond professional? If so, a Municipal Bond Mutual Fund may be the answer.

There are now hundreds of these funds. Some only invest in the bonds of a single state. These give investors in that state the advantage of interest that is free from state and local taxes as well as from federal taxes.

Some funds invest in bonds with short-term maturities to reduce the risk from interest rate fluctuations. Others seek to maximize the amount of current income by lengthening the average maturity of the fund's portfolio. In short, there's probably a fund to match almost any municipal bond strategy you desire.

Why buy a mutual fund at all? Why not just buy individual bonds? I can think of at least two good reasons to prefer a mutual fund over individual bonds. The first has to do with diversification. A mutual fund has the advantage of spreading your investment over a wide variety of bonds. Since municipal bonds come in denominations of $5,000, this diversification is clearly more difficult for those with limited amounts to invest.

The second, perhaps more important advantage of a mutual fund is the value of professional management. Mutual fund managers have demonstrated track records of being able to adjust their portfolios for changes in interest rates. They're able to shorten maturities to reduce the negative effects of increases in interest rates. They're also able to lengthen maturities to take advantage of decreases in interest rates. Most individual investors, from my experience, haven't been nearly so successful.

These advantages do come with a price tag. Mutual

fund companies charge management fees against the value of the funds they're managing. Management fees are generally within the 0.5% - 1.3% range per year. In my view, it's well worth paying these fees for the advantages I've listed.

6.L.
You Deserve Credit

Foreign Tax Credit

Ratings

Comfort	☺ ☺ ☺ ☺ ☺
Convenience	☺ ☺ ☺
Income & Appreciation	☺
Tax Savings	☺
Sex Appeal	☺ ☺

The Foreign Tax Credit may not be a very significant item for most people. When it applies, however, it shouldn't be overlooked. You may be one of the growing number of people who are looking beyond the borders of the U.S.A. for investment opportunities. You may have invested in some foreign stocks or bonds, for example. Or, even more likely, you may have invested a portion of your portfolio in mutual funds that invest overseas.

Foreign, global and *international* mutual funds have sprung up faster than weeds in your garden. Nearly every mutual fund company has an international fund of some sort. Unlike those annoying garden weeds, however, these funds shouldn't make you cringe. With the superior performance some of these funds have turned in, it's small wonder that smart investors are devoting some of their assets to them.

A curious line appears on these fund statements every year, however. It usually says something like "foreign taxes paid" or simply "foreign taxes." What's happening is that many foreign countries directly tax and withhold a portion of the dividends their country's companies are paying. So if Bullfighter Industries of Spain pays a dividend of $1.00 per share, the Spanish government may tax and withhold $0.15 of that dividend before it is paid to the shareholder — in this case the mutual fund that owns the stock. The mutual fund company then reports that $0.15 per share tax on its mutual fund statement as "foreign taxes paid."

As a shareholder of that mutual fund, the tax came out of the money you have invested in the mutual fund. Through the tax that was withheld on your dividends, you may have helped the Spanish government build new bull fighting arenas. Or perhaps your tax was used to pay some of the medical expenses for one of those gored in the annual running of the bulls in Pamplona. Regardless, our tax laws allow you to get the tax back.

Through the Foreign Tax Credit, you generally get to deduct from your U. S. taxes the amount of taxes that you've paid to foreign countries. Since Spanish taxes were withheld from your dividends, you've paid foreign taxes. You can therefore deduct those taxes from the taxes you owe the U. S. Government. Now, isn't that nice of the Congressional Revenue Hunters?

To take advantage of the Foreign Tax Credit, you'll have to complete a special tax form, Form 1116. The credit will then be carried over to the back of your Form 1040. For more information on the Foreign Tax Credit, you should consult your tax preparer or read IRS Publication 514.

The first thing you ought to do, however, is look at your end-of-year statements from your mutual funds and brokerage accounts. If you see "foreign taxes" listed anywhere there, claim the amount on Form 1116.

(If you paid taxes to countries that don't have diplomatic relations with the U.S., you're out of luck. Those taxes aren't eligible for the Foreign Tax Credit.)

6.M.
Build It And They'll...
Give You Credit

Historic Structure Rehabilitation Credit

Ratings

Comfort	☺ ☺ ☺
Convenience	☺
Income & Appreciation	☺ ☺ ☺
Tax Savings	☺ ☺ ☺ ☺
Sex Appeal	☺ ☺ ☺ ☺ ☺

Know of any old buildings in your area that you especially like? Were they built before 1936? Could they qualify as "historic" structures? And do they need some fixing up?

If so, you could rehabilitate a building and get a tax credit for doing it. Rehabilitating a non-residential building that was built before 1936 could qualify for a 10% Investment Tax Credit for Rehabilitation Property.

If the building you have in mind could be certified as an historic structure, you could get a 20% Tax Credit for fixing it up.

Add a little mortgage money to the mix and you can

leverage that Tax Credit into something even more generous. Borrow 50% of the money for the rehabilitation work, for example, and you'll double the credit on your invested dollars.

Maybe you're a real estate developer, a real estate attorney, a well-heeled and well-diversified investor, or just someone who owns a very old building that you think deserves saving. If so, you should do some homework. Quaint old buildings, filled with the unique styles of bygone eras, are being reclaimed from the wrecking ball across America. You could help retain a piece of history, and make some extra bucks in the process.

The full details of the Historic Structure Rehabilitation Credit are clearly more than I want to get into here. But although this is a very special type of investment, and one that is suitable for only a limited number of people, certain individuals should study it carefully. If you fit the mold of one of the types of people I've mentioned, you should consult a tax professional. It could make the difference between a profitable real estate investment and an unprofitable one.

6.N.
Do Good For A Profit

Affordable Housing Tax Credit

Ratings

Comfort	☺ ☺ ☺ ☺
Convenience	☺ ☺ ☺
Income & Appreciation	☺ ☺
Tax Savings	☺ ☺ ☺ ☺ ☺
Sex Appeal	☺ ☺ ☺ ☺ ☺

If I say the words "low-income housing," you might get the mental picture of a government-built inner-city slum. If that's the case, please turn the channel.

What I'm talking about are housing projects that are in the suburbs and in rural areas. They aren't even government projects. They are privately built and privately managed. The projects' tenants aren't wealthy, but they aren't welfare cases either. Each tenant must meet certain income requirements. Rents can also be raised.

Now brace yourself for one more scary term — limited partnership. There, I've said it. The Red Sea didn't part and lightning bolts didn't zap you. It's true that the decade of the 1980s saw a lot of money lost by a lot of people in a lot of limited partnerships. Nearly everyone I know of who was an active investor during the '80s put some money in limited partnerships. Much of that money was either lost or is still being "worked out."

But, as Robert Stanger wrote in the July 1992 issue of *Louis Rukeyser's Wall Street* (1101 King Street, Ste 400, Alexandria, VA 22314 (800) 892-9702), "Not all limited partnerships are duds. Low-income housing partnerships...have actually lived up to their promise." Stanger reported that of 67 such limited partnerships he studied "until they sold their properties,...all projects gained in value and there were no foreclosures. Plus, investors got a nice little tax break."

Want to know more? Read on.

Every year, the federal government, in conjunction with state and local agencies, allocates tax credits to be used by developers of certain low-income housing projects.

Suppose, for example, that you invest $10,000 in a limited partnership that generates a 15% credit. You'll be able to deduct $1,500 *from your tax bill* each year for up to ten years. That's like getting a 15% per year return on your money, *tax free!*

So what's the problem? Well, for one thing, the project can't be sold for 15 years. The law requires that the units be operated as low-income housing for that long in order to qualify for the tax credits. What does that do to your return? If you're in the highest tax bracket and you get all your money back at the end of 15 years, but nothing more, the rate of return will be about 12%. Even if the properties are worthless, your return is still about 8%, excluding your write-off on the loss. Once you add that in, your rate of return jumps up to about 10%. Remember, we're talking about *tax-free* returns here.

You should consider several things before you invest in these programs, however. Affordable housing limited partnerships are extremely illiquid. In other words, once you've invested your money, you aren't likely to be able to cash in your investment. You'll probably get your share of tax credits during the life of the partnership, but nothing more. At the end of the partnership, 15 years or so after you've made your initial investment, you'll also get your share of the proceeds from the sale of the properties. But that's it. There won't be any periodic cash payments along the way.

In short, your benefits from an affordable housing limited partnership are generally limited to the money you may make when the properties are sold and the tax credits generated. As a result, you'd better be sure that you're going to have a steady stream of taxes to offset with the credits during the 10-12 years that you'll get them. If you have a year or more during the life of the partnership in which you don't have enough taxes due to use up the credits, then the credits will be wasted. That will reduce your rate of return and should be avoided.

Let's make this a little simpler. Examine your income tax situation for the next 10-12 years (the help of a tax professional should be useful here). Suppose you forecast that the lowest your tax bill will be during those years is $3,750. If the partnership projects a maximum of 15% in credits in any given year, then the maximum you should invest is your $3,750 in likely taxes due divided by 15%, i.e. $3,750/.15 = $25,000. So $25,000 is the most you should invest. Investing more would result in potentially wasted tax credits.

You may be a high income earner who's laughing at only $3,750 in taxes. Suppose your tax bill is a lot higher than that and that it's likely to stay very high for the next 10-12 years or more. The law says that you can only use tax credits to offset the taxes due on the last $25,000 of your income, regardless of your tax bracket. So there's a maximum amount of credits you can use. And that translates into a maximum amount of investment that you should make in these partnerships. Look at the table on the next page. Based on your tax bracket, you can find the maximum that you should consider investing in a particular partnership.

Do Good For A Profit

Taxable Income	Tax Bracket		Max.Credit Allowed/Yr		Tax Credit Yield*		Maximum Investment
$25,000	X 28.0%	=	$7,000	/	15%	=	$47,000
$25,000	X 31.0%	=	$7,750	/	15%	=	$52,000
$25,000	X 36.0%	=	$9,000	/	15%	=	$60,000
$25,000	X 39.6%	=	$9,900	/	15%	=	$66,000

* The Tax Credit Yield is the maximum amount of tax credits generated by a partnership in any one year. Different percentages will apply to different partnerships.

(These limits only apply to individuals. If you are a "C" corporation, there's no limit on the amount of tax credits that you can use.)

To be prudent, I think you should only consider investing with a partnership sponsor (general partner) that has many years of experience in low-income housing projects. Making sure the properties retain their eligibility for the tax credits can be a complicated task. If the number of qualified tenants falls below a certain minimum amount, for example, the partnership can lose some of its tax credits. So an experienced general partner is essential.

Finally, look for a partnership that's invested in several properties that are spread out over several locations. Heavy concentration in one area can be disastrous. Just think what might have happened if you owned a partnership that was only invested in the path of Hurricane Andrew (or the California earthquakes, or the 1993 midwest floods, etc.). Diversification by location is a key to reducing risk.

7

How To Save Money

The TV blares "Buy, Buy, Buy" in a thousand different ways. Magazines invite you to "share the good life." Newspaper ads tell you that you "deserve" to own this or that.

"Buy now, pay later!" Not only are we encouraged to spend our own money, we're also told to borrow somebody else's money and spend that, too. That's The American Way.

As a result, perhaps, failing to reach financial independence is also The American Way. Studies over the past quarter century have revealed an unbudging statistic. Over 90% of all Americans fail to reach financial independence before they retire. This huge percentage of the population becomes dependent upon three sources of income for survival:

- Social Security, which we all know is very inadequate, and getting more so.

- Welfare, which is inadequate, at best, and totally

dehumanizing, at worst.

• Relatives, who are struggling, both financially and emotionally in most cases, just to provide for themselves.

So how should you prevent yourself from becoming part of the 90+%? First, resist the temptation to borrow to spend. Try to live within your means. Pay off any expensive consumer debt you might have.
Now you're ready to follow my:
Five Steps For Financial Freedom:

1. **Pay yourself first**. Every dollar that flows through your hands should have a portion set aside for investment in your future. Better yet, set the portion aside before the dollar flows through your hands. How much? I think that 10% of all you earn will generally be required and adequate.

2. **Do it now**. Procrastination is among the leading causes of failure to achieve financial independence. Time is your most important ally. Use it.

3. **Set financial goals**. I think it's almost impossible to hit a target unless you're shooting at it. Get specific. Define in terms of time and dollars what

you're trying to achieve. "I want to retire in 22 years with an income, in today's dollars, of $28,000. And I want the money to last until I'm at least 90 years old." That's specific, both in terms of time and dollars.

4. **Develop a plan and monitor your progress.** Once you've set your financial goals, you should develop a specific plan to achieve them. "I'll save 8% of every paycheck. I'll invest that money in a Tax-Smart way and follow the *Five Steps For Comfortable Investing* (from Chapter 2 — Understanding Risk). I'll review my progress toward my goal every year and make adjustments as needed." Now *do* it!

5. **Invest in a Tax-Smart way.** The tax laws allow you to set aside a lot of money tax-deferred and tax-free. If you take advantage of these opportunities, you'll be able to achieve your goals with only about 75% of the savings that you'll need if you ignore them. In fact, ignoring these tax-smart savings opportunities could spell the difference between success and failure in achieving your goals.

You'll also need to develop a certain state of mind to achieve financial independence — a state of mind that's in direct contrast to the immediate gratification mentality that slick consumer advertising promotes so enticingly. You need to understand that success is not achieved quickly. Following the *Five Steps For Financial Freedom* over a period of many years will take you much closer to your goal than trying to hit it big or quickly.

Frequently I hear people say that all they need to do is "get a break," "hit the lottery," or some other unlikely possibility. Most fast methods of achieving financial success come with high risk. And most simply fail to work.

If you've developed the habit of paying yourself first, success is very achievable. You may be expecting a Christmas bonus or an income tax refund, for example. Most people will develop plans long in advance to spend it. You, on the other hand, realize that you haven't needed it this far for living expenses. So "why spend it?" you ask yourself. Instead, you decide to save all of it. You'll set it aside and let time and the magic of compounding do their jobs.

You can do the same with other one-time lumps of money. Aunt Minnie may give you a cash gift. You may inherit some money. A profit-sharing bonus may come your way. Smartly, you realize that you haven't needed this money in the past. So you add it to the money you've previously set aside to achieve your long-term financial goals.

How about pay raises? Your paycheck increases $200. Have you needed that $200 in the past? Really needed it? OK, enjoy some of the raise. Don't make your life miserable. But set aside a significant portion of each raise. This is painless savings since you've been living without the money anyway.

All of these steps are possible. You **can** do them. To do them, all you really need to do is to have the state of mind that you **will** do them.

There's another point that you should keep in mind. I think that it's much easier to save money if you've never gotten your hands on it. That's why the government requires you to withhold taxes from your paycheck (those Congressional Revenue Hunters may be nasty, but they're not stupid). Similarly, employer-sponsored investment plans like 401(k)s and 403(b)s are payroll deductions. Use these plans as much as you can.

What about money you need to set aside that can't come out of your paycheck? Try to make it as automatic as possible. You may already pay your mortgage or your utility bills with an automatic debit from your bank checking account. Why not do the same for your investments? Many of the investment vehicles I've discussed have plans that allow you to invest through an automatic monthly or quarterly withdrawal from your bank account. Take advantage of these plans.

If payroll deductions and debits against bank accounts aren't enough, then try to physically and emotionally segregate your savings from your living expense money. Establish separate investment accounts with a bank, brokerage firm, mutual fund family, insurance company, etc. Set aside some money from every paycheck into one or more of these accounts. This will take care of the physical segregation of the money.

You'll also need to emotionally segregate your investment money. Except for your annual progress monitoring reviews, you must put your investment money out of your mind. Why? To avoid self-destructing.

I've had the opportunity to help a great number of people along the road to financial freedom. They've established goals and developed realistic plans to achieve those goals. They've set aside money for investments and invested wisely. Their nest eggs grew to sizable amounts. Then some of them self-destructed.

Their assets had grown to significant amounts. Then they **noticed it**. The money sparked the dreams that lead to self-destruction. "I hate my boss," some said. "I'm going to use my investment money to buy a business." Far too often, the business they bought was one they didn't adequately understand. While it may have relieved the "hated boss" problem, it replaced it with the "we can't make our business work" problem. Soon, they were left with a bitter experience and no investment money.

Other times I've witnessed people lose sight of their goals and what it takes to achieve them. Their investment nest egg had grown considerably. Then they yielded to the temptation to spend the money on something big. That world cruise they'd long dreamed of now looked possible. The boat they'd always wanted came sailing into their imaginations. They started mentally decorating the mountain cabin they'd wanted since they were kids. Poof! The investments got blown away from their intended goals.

Now, I certainly am not telling you not to dream, not to have financial goals outside of retirement planning. What I am saying is that you shouldn't use your retirement nest egg to fund these other dreams and goals.

"We'll be alright," some will say. "We've done pretty well, so far. We can put the money back later." Please forgive me for saying it, but I really have heard all this before. And you know what? It's all nothing more than an attempt to rationalize getting off the plan, ignoring the goal — self-destructing.

So pay attention to these impulses if they strike you.

Recognize them for what they are. Resist these urges and stay with your plan. If you do, you **will** succeed.

8

There's No Free Lunch

An Observation About Commissions, Fees, Sales Charges, Etc.

I've always been amazed at a paradox in the investment world. On the one hand, many people seem to be willing to pay an enormous amount of money for publications that offer to provide the impossible — accurate predictions about the future. At the same time, these same people seem to be *un*willing to pay a financial professional a modest fee to advise them about their investments and to guide them to appropriate solutions to their financial problems.

Investment publications spring up in offices, upstairs bedrooms, basements and garages across the land. All it takes, it seems, is a computer, some word processing and spreadsheet software, and a mailing list of would-be subscribers and voilá, you're in the investment newsletter business.

Never mind that the advice from one newsletter is in sharp contrast to the advice from another. Never mind that the recommendations are based on "financial statement analysis," "momentum analysis," "trend analysis," and the charting of "head and shoulders patterns" — everything, it seems, from tea leaves to the phases of the moon form the basis for investment advice. Never mind that investment advisory newsletter opinions are a relatively reliable *contrary* indicator of which way the investment markets will go. The fact is that tens of thousands of people spend millions of dollars on scores of newsletters that seem to promise to do the impossible — namely, predict the future.

And wow, what a wad of money these predictions cost! How about *The Hickory 250* at $135 for 12 issues? Or *The Utility Forecaster*, for only $109 for 12 issues? Or *ProFiles Fax Service* which will shower you with 250 issues, but at a cold water dousing price of $450.

Hey, want a niche market? There's the *California Technology Stock Letter*, an even two dozen issues for $295. Want only good stuff? There's *Investment Quality Trends* at $275 for 24 issues. In what direction is the market headed? Try *The Primary Trend* at $180 for 12 issues.

What does Andrew Addison think? How about John Schott, Louis Ehrenkrantz, Philip Ruta, or Alan Lancz? They'll be glad to tell you in newsletters that bear their names — *The Addison Report*, *The Schott Letter*, *The Ehrenkrantz Report*, *The Ruta Financial Newsletter*, *The Lancz Letter*, you get the picture — all available at lofty prices. But who are these guys? And why would you pay real cash to know what they think?

The Prudent Speculator sells 12 issues for $175. A prudent speculator? Isn't that like a jumbo shrimp?

There's No Free Lunch

Don't you love *Overpriced Stock Service* at $495 for 12 issues?! Hey, *they* labeled it "overpriced," not me! And finally, there's *The Quiet Investor* that gives you 12 issues for only $60. I think I'll just quietly invest my $60 elsewhere.

I don't mean to pick on any of these publications, or the people who produce them. Heck, if I didn't think *some* financial planning publications were worth paying for, I wouldn't be writing this book, would I?! I'm just amazed, however, at the people I've known who spend over $1,000 a year on newsletters to guide them in managing investment portfolios of less than $20,000. That's spending over 5% of your investment dollars per year on advice from people *who have never met you and know nothing about you!*.

That's the paradox. These same people seem to have an instinctive aversion to listening to the advice of a financial professional.

I don't get it. Would they really rather spend 5% of their investment money *every year* on newsletters of questionable validity than spend 5% *one time* on a mutual fund commission. "Why pay a commission when you don't have to?" they'll ask. To me, a *one time* commission, paid to a financial professional who knows you and can guide you toward your goals, is a far better deal than spending lots of money, *year after year*, on crystal ball gazing publications that may not even relate to your unique circumstances.

Perhaps one explanation is that this is the age of self-help and the do-it-yourselfer. Self reliance can be an admirable quality, but taken to the extreme, we would need no professionals of any kind! Remember the adage that "a lawyer who represents himself has a fool for a client?" How many doctors will treat members of their own families?

Now, you may be the best bio-chemist in the world. Or perhaps you've become the most educated and experienced psychologist who ever lived. But does that give you what you need to know to make intelligent, informed decisions on your own about investments? Don't you rely on other professionals for advice on lots of issues outside your own education and experience?

What about your time? Most people tell me their work is a full-time matter. Add to that the time you need to devote to family matters. Do you really expect to do justice to your financial affairs by merely squeezing in a little time now and then? Don't your investments deserve more attention than that?

Another explanation for people not wanting to pay for professional financial advice may be confusion over what constitutes a financial professional. It's true, some financial professionals may have masters degrees, some are CPAs, some are tax attorneys, insurance agents, brokers — and some wear several of these hats.

There's No Free Lunch

It *can* seem confusing. However, don't focus solely on titles or degrees. Look for education, yes, but also experience, a good track record, and satisfied clients.

Don't know where to look for a financial professional? I suggest the *referral route*. Ask your friends, relatives and business associates who they've used. Ask them whether they're satisfied with the advice and service they've gotten. Or ask your accountant or attorney. If these fail, try the yellow pages.

In any case, be sure to interview financial professionals until you find one who's genuinely interested in your financial situation. Does the person have suggestions that he or she will explain in a way you can understand? Are you comfortable with the suggestions? If so, you've found a financial professional with whom you can work. You're a fortunate person, because you've taken the time to find someone who can guide you through a lifetime of investing.

Now, use that person's advice. Reward that person with your continuing business. And share your good fortune by giving that person's name to your friends so they can be just as fortunate as you are.

But don't abuse the relationship by taking the advice from your financial professional and then doing the business somewhere else where the fees are slightly cheaper. How will the financial professional stay in business if people do that? How will he or she be there for future advice and service?

I've known literally hundreds of brokers, financial planners and insurance agents, and they have at least one common characteristic. They're generally very loyal to clients who are loyal to them. They'll go out of their way to help clients who continue to do business with them.

So remember, like you, your financial professional is working for a living. And by working together, you can help each other prosper!

"You can marry for love.
You can marry for fun.
If you get a little money
along with it,
don't complain!"
— Anon.

Epilogue

There are three things you can do with your money.

1. Own Things With Your Money

You can invest in businesses at home and abroad that produce goods and services. You can own their stocks directly or through mutual funds.

You can own capital, like buildings, equipment and real estate.

You can own works of art, antiques, precious metals and gemstones.

Most of these will produce a variable rate of return. Though variable, that rate will probably exceed the fixed rate of return available on other investments.

2. Lend Your Money To Those Who Own Things

You can lend money to banks, savings and loans, corporations or governments. They'll turn around and use your money to buy things you're afraid to buy and lend to people you're afraid to lend to. You'll make money, but they'll probably make more money with your money than you'll make with it.

3. Spend Your Money

If you do this, you'll prevent yourself from doing the first two things.

Appendix A

Final Value Of An
IRA Investment

*Comparison of Taxable Investment vs. Deductible IRA
vs. Non-Deductible IRA
For 28% & 36% Tax-Bracket Taxpayers*

Assumptions:

Annual Contribution to the IRA	$ 2,000
Rate of Return on the IRA Investment	10%

Yr	Taxable Investment 28%	36%	Deductible IRA 28%	36%	Non-Deductible IRA 28%	36%
0	1,440	1,280	2,000	2,000	1,440	1,280
1	2,984	2,642	4,200	4,200	3,024	2,688
2	4,639	4,091	6,620	6,620	4,766	4,236
3	6,412	5,633	9,282	9,282	6,682	5,939
4	8,314	7,273	12,210	12,210	8,790	7,812
5	10,353	9,019	15,431	15,431	11,109	9,873
10	22,971	19,572	37,060	37,060	26,679	23,713
15	40,834	33,963	71,894	71,894	51,755	46,002
20	66,123	53,588	127,995	127,995	92,141	81,900
25	101,925	80,849	218,345	218,345	157,183	139,713
30	152,611	116,842	363,853	363,853	261,934	232,822
After-tax	152,611	116,842	261,974	232,866	200,688	162,830

Ready, Set, Retire!

Acknowledgments

Where do I start? There are so many people to thank for their help.

Dave Chilton inspired me with his book, *The Wealthy Barber*, and his speaking career. More than anything, though, he's been a valuable resource person for me. He's selflessly spent time initiating me into the world of public speaking and publishing. His encouragement helped me to continue this pursuit when I might otherwise have quit.

Jean Russell Nave, an accomplished public speaker and author, helped open my eyes to the possibilities of this work. She also read parts of the book and provided valuable comments to make it better.

Alden Olsen, Professor of Finance at Michigan State University, always shared his many insights. His advice was instrumental in guiding me into a career in the investment world.

Jim Brinkley, President of Legg Mason, Inc., identified my strengths years ago. He helped me to see that my career should be as an author and public speaker.

John Prokopchak, Senior Vice President of Capital Financial Group/H. Beck, Inc., has been unfailing in his faith in me. His encouragement and support at a critical point in this project enabled me to carry it to completion.

Jim Mitchell, a friend of long standing, offered valuable insights into the world of book publishing.

His selfless help smoothed what could have been a very bumpy road.

Don Roose, loyal client and cherished friend, has always been supportive. His editorial comments helped make this a better book.

Lisa Sheehan, friend and fellow adventurer, provided her expert editorial input. If you find this book to be a good read, Lisa deserves a big part of the credit. If not, the blame is mine.

Nancy Records Allen, a member of my company's staff, has provided emotional support from the very beginning. She's also given her time and talent to the creation and production of this book.

Similarly, Joyce Davis has been a loyal assistant. Through good times and rough times, she's hung in there with her sharp wit and get-it-done efficiency.

My wife, Cathy, who's seen me through a lot of ups and downs over the years, has been even more supportive than usual with this project. She deserves the rewards the project will bring.

My children, Christie and Scott, have sacrificed more than they understand. I hope the success of this project will allow me to give them more of the Daddy time they deserve.

Lynn and Jay Hill, former next door neighbors and now lifelong friends, have given us their heads, hands and hearts more often than we have the right to expect.

Acknowledgments

Thousands of clients and acquaintances, whose names must remain confidential, have shared with me their personal financial concerns. I'm very grateful to them, since it was through helping them achieve their goals that I've gained the experience and many of the insights I needed to write this book.

James Berger, President of TMI Tax Services, 923 Mainstreet, Hopkins, MN 55343, allowed me to use extensive excerpts from *Income Tax & Financial Planning Quickfinder Handbook (Form 1040) 1994 Edition - 1993 Tax Year.* Tax preparers, financial planners and anyone else in the financial services industry would be well advised to own the most recent copy of this excellent, annually-updated handbook.

Louis Rukeyser's Wall Street, 1101 King Street, Suite 400, Alexandria, VA 22314, (800) 892-9702, allowed me to use excerpts from July 1992, Vol. 1, Number 5, about affordable housing partnerships.

*"Who said a glossary
has to be a boring
list of words
and terms?"*
— *J. Wm. Brimacombe*

Glossary

Aardvark: This isn't really a term that applies to retirement or investments. I just like the sound of it.

Account Executive: One of several brokerage industry terms for Broker.

Affordable Housing: This refers to a special kind of housing project that meets the requirement of the tax laws. Such projects can provide investors with attractive rates of return and tax advantages. These projects are usually offered to investors in the form of limited partnership interests. See Chapter 6.N. — Do Good For A Profit.

Annuity: A contract with an insurance company that allows an investor to invest tax-deferred, in virtually any amount for almost any length of time during the investor's lifetime. Annuities come in a variety of forms, including single-premium and flexible-premium contracts. The rates of return earned on the money invested in an annuity can be either fixed or variable, depending upon the contract selected. See Chapter 6.E. — The Topless IRA.

Attorney: Someone who practices law. Although some attorneys are tax professionals, many attorneys are not. To find out, ask if they specialize in tax matters.

Banker: Someone in the business of borrowing from you (in the form of deposits) at a low rate of interest and lending to you (in the form of credit card loans, auto loans, consumer loans, business loans, etc.) at high rates of interest. It's surprising, I think, that some bankers actually lose money doing this.

Bonds: A financial instrument that says the issuer of the bond will pay the holder(i.e. owner) of the bond a specific amount of interest at a specific time each year, plus the face amount of the bond at a specific maturity date. If the issuer goes bankrupt, the bond holders will get paid their share of anything that's left before the stock holders get anything. Also, see Chapter 6.K. — Tax-Free in Four Flavors.

Bond Call: If a bond has a "call" feature, the issuer will have the right to call, or buy back, the bond at a specific price at a specified time prior to the maturity date.   See Chapter 6.K.1. — Municipal Bonds - Same State as Residence.

Broker: Someone through whom you can buy and sell securities. Also variously known as stockbroker, investment broker, financial consultant, account executive, registered representative, investment executive, and financial planner. See also Financial Professional.   Also, see Chapter 8 — There's No Free Lunch.

Brokerage Firm: A company in the business of buying and selling securities, advising clients on how to achieve their investment goals, and managing financial assets.

Capital Gains: When the value of a capital asset (stocks, bonds, real estate, other assets held for investment purposes) rises in value, it is called a capital gain. A capital gain is taxed differently (often, at a lower rate) than ordinary income.   See Chapter 6.F. — The Good Got Better and

Chapter 6.G. — Good Enough To Die For.

CD: See Certificate of Deposit.

Certificate of Annuity: These are fixed-rate annuities with relatively short maturities, usually of one to five years.

Certificate of Deposit: Also known as a CD. An account at a bank that pays a fixed rate of interest for a fixed amount of time. The CD may or may not be federally insured, depending on whether the issuing bank is insured.

Certified Financial Planner: A Financial Planner who has taken a series of home-study or in-class courses and passed a certification examination on material related to financial planning. Also, see Chapter 8 — There's No Free Lunch.

Certified Public Accountant (CPA): Someone who has passed the rigorous examination to become a Certified Public Accountant. Also, someone who practices public accounting. Someone who is generally qualified to render tax advice and/or prepare tax returns. A CPA may be a tax professional if he or she specializes in taxation matters.

CFP: See Certified Financial Planner.

Client: That's you from the point of view of a Broker, Financial Planner, Insurance Agent, or Banker.

Comfortable: Your comfort zone in terms of where you invest your capital, with whom, and the risks you take to see it grow. If you are *comfortable* with how your money is invested, you will likely leave it there and let it perform in the way it was intended. If you are *un*comfortable, you'll likely disrupt the financial plan upon which you've embarked, thereby preventing you from achieving the plan's goals.

Commissions: This is one form of compensation for Financial Professionals (e.g. Bankers, Brokers, Financial Planners and Insurance Agents). Expressed as a percentage of the Client's investment or insurance premium, the commission is split among the Financial Professional, the company for whom the Financial Professional works, and the company issuing or sponsoring the investment or insurance vehicle.

Common Stock: See Stock.

Congressional Revenue Hunters: These are members of the U.S. Congress. They are much like some deer hunters I know. There's an annual session of Congress, like there's a season for deer hunting. They often attack unlikely targets with threats of taxation. In their floundering around, they frequently miss the target they say they're shooting at. In the process, they inflict a lot of damage on innocents, like cattle that looked like deer through beer-blurred eyes. They never tire of their work, so they come back year after year. To some, it's like a game — a great sport. The committee hearings and floor debates charge their souls. Others do it for "the good of the country" like those who shoot deer for their meat. What they bring home, however, is frequently foul tasting stuff that nobody's proud of. Meanwhile, like the sparkle of life that leaves the big, brown eyes of the deer, the innate optimism of the American spirit often leaves the hearts of the frequently frustrated American taxpayer.

CPA: See Certified Public Accountant.

Deduction: See Tax Deduction.

Deferral: See Tax Deferral.

Discount Broker: A brokerage firm that offers reduced brokerage commissions in exchange for reduced service.

Diversification: Spreading your money among a variety of investments. To deal with uncertainty, prudent investors invest in a number of different investments to reduce their risk. Also, see Chapter 2 — Understanding Risk.

Dividend: The amount of money a company distributes in cash to its shareholders.

Face Value: The amount that a bond or other debt obligation promises to pay its holder at maturity. This is not the same as Market Value.

Fee: One form of compensation for Bankers, Brokers, Financial Planners and Insurance Agents. Fees can be either flat amounts charged to Clients periodically (quarterly, etc.) or amounts expressed as a percentage of the amount invested or the amount being managed. See also Commissions.

Financial Consultant: One who advises people about their financial affairs. Also, one of several brokerage industry terms for Broker.

Financial Planner: Someone who can help you develop a plan to achieve your financial goals.

Financial Professional: Someone with a background in financial matters who offers investment advice for compensation. This includes Bankers, Brokers, Financial Planners and Insurance Agents, and sometimes accountants and attorneys. Also, see Chapter 8 — There's No Free Lunch.

Fixed Annuity: An annuity that offers a fixed versus a variable rate of return on the money invested in the contract. See Annuity. Also, see Chapter 6.E. — The Topless IRA.

Foreign Tax Credit: Many foreign countries withhold taxes at the source on stocks and bonds issued within their borders. U. S. tax laws allow American taxpayers a credit against U. S. taxes for any such foreign taxes paid. See Chapter 6.L. — You Deserve Credit.

Head and Shoulders: The pattern of a stock's price movements when a stock has risen three times from a level where it seems to go no lower. Also, a brand of shampoo. The shampoo is probably more useful to investors.

Hot: As in *Hot tip*, an investment idea that is usually neither hot nor much of a tip; something that only novice investors take seriously. As in *Hot issue*, a newly issued stock that has stimulated a lot of buying interest. As the Wall Street axiom says, "if it's a great stock, you won't be able to get any of it. If it's NOT a great stock, you'll be able to get all you want." So, if you can get a lot of it, you probably shouldn't want it. As in *buying something Hot*, a way novice investors invariably get burned.

HR10 Plan: See Keogh Plan. Also, see Chapter 6.B. — Alphabet Soup to Warm Your Retirement.

Immediate Annuity: An annuity that offers an immediate, fixed, periodic payment based on several factors, including the amount of money invested in the contract and the age and sex of the person receiving the payment. See Annuity. See Chapter 6.E. — The Topless IRA.

Individual Retirement Account: An account with a financial institution that allows a taxpayer to accumulate retirement money tax-deferred. The tax laws set a variety of limitations and conditions on these accounts. See Chapter

Glossary

6.A. — Good Things Come in Small Packages.

Inflation: Inflation is when prices go up without any additional goods or services being provided. It is the silent killer of Purchasing Power.

Insurance Agent: One who sells insurance policies. See Financial Professional. Also, see Chapter 8 — There's No Free Lunch.

Insured: This is a term that is often used rather loosely in the financial community. It usually refers to some sort of third-party promise to pay if a security issuer defaults on its obligations to pay interest and/or principal. If an investment security is federally insured, it will say so. Otherwise, it is probably insured by some other organization, like a consortium of insurance companies (these are common in the Municipal Bond area). It is also a common misunderstanding to think that securities are insured when they're sold by an organization that has other insured accounts. Mutual funds sold by banks, for example, are not insured any more than mutual funds sold by brokers. The security itself must be insured.

Interest Rate: This shouldn't be confused with Return on Investment. Interest is only a part of the Return on Investment for many investments. It is the amount of money that a bond, CD, etc. will periodically pay its holders. It is expressed in terms of a percentage of the investment. For example, a $1,000 investment that will pay $100 in cash every year has an interest rate of $100/$1000 = 10%. If the value of the underlying $1,000 goes up to $1,200, then there is also a Capital Gain of $200 in addition to the

Interest of $100. So the total Return on Investment is Capital Gain + Interest = $200 + $100. Expressed as a percentage of the original investment we have ($200 + $100)/$1,000 = 30%.

Investment Broker: One of several brokerage industry terms for Broker. See Broker. Also, see Chapter 8 — There's No Free Lunch.

IRA: See Individual Retirement Account.

Keogh Plan: A type of retirement plan available to sole proprietorships and partnerships. Though complicated, Keogh Plans can be excellent for those who want to tax-defer a lot of income and have the money to do it. See Chapter 6.B. — Alphabet Soup to Warm Your Retirement.

Lawyer: See Attorney.

Life Insurance Policy: A contract with an insurance company to pay named beneficiaries a sum of money if the insured person dies. It provides a pool of assets that will generate income to replace the income that was provided by the deceased while alive. Also used to pay estate taxes upon the death of the insured. Certain types of Life Insurance Policies can also be used to fund a retirement plan. See Chapter 6.C. — Cut The Red Tape, and Chapter 6.J. — The Jackpot.

Load: A sales charge on a mutual fund. See No-Load. Also, see Chapter 8 — There's No Free Lunch.

Low-Income Housing: See Affordable Housing. Also, see Chapter 6.N. — Do Good For A Profit.

Management Fees: The expenses of running a mutual fund deducted from the value of the securities portfolio being managed. Since it's not an add-on charge, mutual fund investors are frequently unaware of it.

Market Value: The amount that a security could be sold for now. For a bond, the market value is usually expressed as a percentage of the Face Value of the bond. E.g. a Market Value of 99.5 would be 99.5% of the Face Value.

Municipal Bond: A Bond that is issued by a state, municipality, or some other political subdivision of a state. A Municipal Bond pays interest that is considered tax-free. A same-state municipal bond is issued within the same state as the taxpayer's residence. As such, a same-state municipal bond is free of taxation from both the federal government and the taxpayer's state government and any local government within that state. Such a bond is considered Triple-Tax-Free, i.e. federal, state and local. See Bond and Tax-Free. Also, see Chapter 6.K. — Tax-Free In Four Flavors.

Mutual Fund: A mutual fund pools the investment dollars from many investors. The fund's portfolio manager(s) invests these dollars in a variety of securities in an effort to achieve the objectives outlined in the fund's prospectus. In this way, a mutual fund provides a method of investing. A mutual fund provides investors with: Professional management, diversification, small investment amounts, readily available liquidity, investment flexibility and easy reinvestment of dividends, interest and capital gains.

No-Load: Refers to a mutual fund sold without a Load, or sales charge, but not without management fees. Since management fees may be substantially larger than those for many Load funds, a long-term No-Load fund investor may pay more money over time in management fees than a Load fund investor pays in Loads and management fees combined.

Purchasing Power: What your dollars will buy in goods and services. Without inflation, your Purchasing Power will stay constant. With inflation, however, it will take more dollars to buy the same amount of goods and services. The purchasing power of the dollars will shrink. A well devised investment strategy will preserve and even increase the Purchasing Power of the investment, after taxes.

Registered Representative: One of several brokerage industry terms for Broker.

Return on Investment: This is what you get paid for investing your money, and it comes in several forms. Dividends are paid to stock holders out of the earnings of the company. Interest is paid to bond owners and account depositors. Capital gains are from increases in the value of the investment, e.g. when a stock's price goes up. The Return on Investment is the combination of all of these things, and is usually expressed as a percentage of the amount invested. For example, assume you invest $100 in a stock, get dividends during the year of $5, and the stock's price goes up $8 to $108. You divide the $5 dividend plus the $8 price rise by the $100 you invested: ($5 + $8)/$100 = 13%. So your Return on Investment is 13%.

Revenue Hunters: See Congressional Revenue Hunters.

Risk: The *Purchasing Power* definition of risk that's used in this book is as follows: *Risk is the possibility that an investment will give us less future purchasing power than we started with, after deducting taxes and the effects of infla-*

Glossary

tion. See Chapter 2 — Understanding Risk.

S.E.C.: The Securities and Exchange Commission, the U.S. Government organization charged with regulating all securities markets and transactions in securities.

SEP Plan: A Simplified Employee Pension (SEP) is an IRA or a group of IRAs in which the employer contributes to the IRAs on behalf of its employees. The chief advantage of a SEP is its simplicity. See Chapter 6.B. — Alphabet Soup to Warm Your Retirement.

Series EE: These are bonds issued by the U. S. Treasury that offer tax-deferral of income for those seeking investments that are small in size and safe in terms of loss of principal or interest. See Chapter 6.H. — Better Than Underwear On Christmas Morning.

Series HH: Like Series EE bonds, Series HH bonds are issued by the U. S. Treasury. Series HH bonds are used when a person wants to cash in Series EE bonds and reinvest the proceeds into something that will pay current income but will continue the deferral of income tax on the accumulated Series EE bond interest. See Chapter 6.H. — Better Than Underwear On Christmas Morning.

Stock: A share in the ownership of a company. A company's stockholders are its owners.

Stockbroker: See Broker.

Stock Dividend: A distribution from a company to its shareholders in the form of company stock.

Tax Credit: A dollar for dollar reduction in the amount of taxes you must pay. E.g. a tax credit of $100 will offset $100 in taxes that would otherwise have to be paid. See also Chapter 6.L. — You Deserve Credit, Chapter 6.M. — Build It And They'll...Give You Credit, and Chapter 6.N. — Do Good For A Profit.

Tax Deduction: An item that you can use on your tax return to reduce the amount of taxes that you must pay. See all parts of Chapter 6.

Tax-Deferral: Tax-Deferral is when the payment of taxes is postponed until a later date.

Tax-Deferred Annuity: See Annuity. Also, see Chapter 6.E. — The Topless IRA.

Tax-Free: Not subject to income tax. An investment that is said to be tax-free is usually free from federal income taxation. A triple-tax-free security is also free from state and local income taxation.

Tax Professional: Someone trained in taxation who offers tax advice and/or prepares tax returns. Usually an accountant, CPA, or an attorney who specializes in taxes.

Tax-Shelter: An investment that seeks to protect investors from taxes. That goal of protection from taxes is usually subject to the whims of the Congressional Revenue Hunters.

TDA: Tax-Deferred Annuity. See Annuity. Also, see Chapter 6.E. — The Topless IRA.

Topless IRA: Tax-Deferred Annuity. See Annuity. Also, see Chapter 6.E. — The Topless IRA.

Treasuries: A general term used for the marketable bills, notes and bonds issued by the U.S. Government. This term isn't usually used to include non-marketable bonds like Series EE and Series HH bonds.

Glossary

Triple-Tax-Free: See Tax-Free and Municipal Bond. Also, see Chapter 6.K. — Tax-Free in Four Flavors.

TSA: Tax-Sheltered Annuity or 403(b) Plan. See Annuity. Also, see Chapter 6.B. — Alphabet Soup to Warm Your Retirement.

Unit Investment Trust: A group of bonds, wrapped up in a single package, and sold in units. The bonds are selected by bond professionals to meet specified interest rate, risk and maturity criteria. They come in a variety of maturities. See Chapter 6.K.3. — Tax-Free in Four Flavors - Municipal Bond Unit Investment Trusts.

Universal Life Insurance Policy: This is a life insurance policy that, in addition to paying your heirs money when you die, can be used to accumulate money tax-deferred for use during retirement, etc. See Chapter 6.C. — Cut the Red Tape and Chapter 6.J. — The Jackpot.

Variable Annuity: An annuity that offers a variable rate of return on the money invested in the contract. See Annuity. Also, see Chapter 6.E. — The Topless IRA.

Variable Universal Life Insurance: In essence, it is mutual funds inside a life insurance policy wrapper. It offers the growth potential of mutual funds combined with the tax-deferred growth and tax-free income benefits of an insurance policy. See Chapter 6.J. — The Jackpot.

Yield: The interest rate on an investment security, expressed as a percentage of the market value of that security. E. g. a bond that pays $50 per year on a market value of $1,000 has a 50/1000 = 5% current yield.

401(k): An employer sponsored retirement plan that allows employees to deduct a percentage of their pre-tax income and have it invested in a tax-deferred retirement account. See Chapter 6.B. — Alphabet Soup to Warm Your Retirement.

403(b): An employer sponsored retirement plan, similar to a 401(k), for employees of tax-exempt organizations. See Chapter 6.B. — Alphabet Soup to Warm Your Retirement.

Index

Index

Index

Index

Index

Ready, Set, Retire!

How Much Money You Need
&
The TAX-SMART Way To Get It & Keep It

Isn't there someone you know who would benefit from *Ready, Set, Retire!?* It's the perfect gift for everyone between the ages of 18 and 108. It's filled with information, fun to read, and profitable!

Please rush me _____ copies of *Ready, Set, Retire!* at $24.99 each. **We pay shipping.** I have enclosed a check made payable to Financial Security Corporation in the amount of $_____.

Full Name:_____

Address:_____

City:_____ State:_____

Zip Code:_____

Telephone#:_____

We offer a discount for volume orders. Please write to us for details, or call us at 1-800-382-6936. Visa and MasterCard orders accepted by phone.

Financial Security Corporation
c/o Financial Freedom Press
P. O. Box 6285
Bend, OR 97708-6285
Tel: (800) 382-6936

Ready, Set, Retire!

How Much Money You Need
&
The TAX-SMART Way To Get It & Keep It

Isn't there someone you know who would benefit from *Ready, Set, Retire!*? It's the perfect gift for everyone between the ages of 18 and 108. It's filled with information, fun to read, and profitable!

Please rush me _____ copies of *Ready, Set, Retire!* at $24.99 each. **We pay shipping.** I have enclosed a check made payable to Financial Security Corporation in the amount of $_____.

Full Name:_____

Address:_____

City:_____ State:_____

Zip Code:_____

Telephone#:_____

We offer a discount for volume orders. Please write to us for details, or call us at 1-800-382-6936. Visa and MasterCard orders accepted by phone.

Financial Security Corporation
c/o Financial Freedom Press
P. O. Box 6285
Bend, OR 97708-6285
Tel: (800) 382-6936